Contents

Contents

Foreword

I was on a visit to Alaska over the Memorial Day weekend. While I was in Anchorage one day, waiting for a bus, an indigenous man in his 50s came up to me with a smile on his face. He told me he could speak many languages. He rattled off the names of a few indigenous languages, one of which I could recognize for sure: "Sugpiaq"; then he proceeded to speak some phrases in one or more of those same languages. I nodded friendlily and, smiling, responded that I too could speak several languages; to act in kind, I proceeded to speak in French to him.

Out of the blue, he then asked me if I "backed the white people." I asked him to repeat the question to be certain I had heard him correctly.

"Do you support the white people?" he said, seriously now.

By this time, I suspected he had been drinking. Being white myself, I told him that I did.

"You support the white people?" he asked again, almost incredulous.

"I am a white person," I admitted. "Why would I not support my own people?" To qualify my comment, I added, "I will always support the good, and fight the bad."

He smiled, but looked offended. I smiled too, and I was not. I felt also that my interpretation of good and bad white people was probably different than his.

Little did he know that I had come to Alaska specifically to learn more about the history and inter-actions among early Russian fur traders and indige-nous peoples, the Aleuts in particular – one of whose languages, Sugpiaq, he spoke.

His bus came, he got on, and our conversation ended. It was too bad for it had great potential for the both of us. My trip to Alaska was nearing its end, and I had been hoping to meet at least one knowledgeable indigenous person of a certain age with whom I could have an intelligent conversation about such topics.

I was neither offended by his prejudice nor ashamed, personally, for what some, perhaps many, white peo-ple have done to indigenous peoples over the course of time. (I am ashamed for humankind sometimes, however.) I felt secure in my knowledge that it was not *I* who committed any wicked act against him or his people; consequently I cannot assume another per-son's guilt. I don't think it works that way. Unless by being white, I must share the guilt of all other white people before me or contemporaneous with me. But if so, that "law" applies to other races too; I don't think anyone wants to be held accountable for some-thing someone else did. Sins of the fathers, and all that...

These days, I'm quite used to some people of color practicing prejudice in the same breath as they accuse white people of racism. Racism is endemic to America, they say, and racism is endemic to white,

Western civilization. Little do they know or care perhaps that it is much more endemic to other, more homogenous societies. They have countless incidents that they can point to, to back up their accusations or feelings. If a person is white, a person is racist, goes the argument. White people, *because* they are white, are all bad actors consequently and all participative in the evil acts of a relative few. If that's not prejudice, and possibly racism, I don't know what is. I'm also used to hearing some people of color say that the only people qualified to understand racism, the only people qualified to identify it and call out acts of racism, are people of color. White people are not qualified.

This may seem like an odd way to begin the foreword to a translation of a book by Léon Bloy about Christopher Columbus and his Cause for Beatification, but it is actually quite germane.

Because the narrative about Christopher Columbus and his incredible, miraculous discovery, that multiple thousands of millions of people have benefited from – a discovery that "doubled the size of the earth" – is anything but straightforward. It is complicated by uncertainties. It is uncertain, for instance, whether he was from Genoa, Spain, or Portugal, originally; it is uncertain whether his native tongue was Genoese, Italian, Spanish, or Portuguese; he wrote his diaries in Spanish apparently, but with indications of non fluency; it is uncertain whether he was a Christian or a converted Jew; the list of uncertainties does not end there; we are awash in uncertainties.

It is not just today that his story and achievements appear complicated. They were complicated days and years before he embarked on his first voyage.

In the same year Columbus set out and discovered the West Indies, – in 1492, – the Spanish crown had issued the Alhambra Decree, which mandated that all Jews who did not convert to Catholicism be expelled from the country. It was a further development of the Inquisition, begun in Spain in 1478, to rid the country of heretics to the Catholic religion. Columbus' interpreter, Luis de Torres, who accompanied him on his first voyage, is said to have been a convert from Judaism. Columbus himself, according to some accounts, is said to have been a convert from Judaism too. If this is true, Léon Bloy either knew nothing about it, or his prior Jewishness did not matter to him – but it may have accounted for the delay then, and to this very day, of Columbus' beatification and canonization.

Nowadays, Columbus is often accused by some people of acting brutally against the indigenous peoples of America. Although it is true that he speaks in his diaries of the possibility of enslaving the population easily – because they were a stone-age people without modern technology or firearms, – there is no hard and fast proof, that I know of, that he himself did it or gave the order. And even if he did, we must be careful not to judge the man or his actions by the "morality of the 20th [or 21st] century."[1] It is important

---

[1]"the morality of the 20th century": Mary Ann Castronovo Fusco, "In Person; In Defense Of Columbus". *The New York Times*. October 8, 2000.

to keep in mind also that indigenous peoples are widely known to have kept slaves themselves, – not just in 1492, but probably much earlier, and also much later – as late as 1805, when Lewis and Clark encountered the indigenous peoples of the Pacific Northwest, along the Columbia River in Oregon territory. In Columbus' diary from the first voyage, some of the very first peoples he meets are said to fear a certain other tribe or nation who often raid them and take slaves from among them. A similar practice of slavery in 18th century Alaska among the Aleuts and other Eskimo peoples is also a known fact. Indigenous peoples practiced slavery amongst themselves, from time immemorial – from North to South Pole, throughout the Americas.

Columbus is often accused of having negligently wiped out entire populations of peoples – a "genocide" contend his detractors – by introducing smallpox and other highly infectious diseases that Europeans were immune to and indigenous peoples were not. The vaccine for smallpox was developed over three hundred years later, in 1796: to charge Columbus with responsibility for the spread of infectious diseases, and not doing anything about it, assuming he knew what was going on in the first place, is about as fair as charging anyone among us in the U.S. or Western Europe of having willfully spread COVID-19 in the winter of 2019. If we were carriers, we did not know it. If we knew it, there was no vaccine: there was nothing we could do about it once the damage was done. Columbus was not Anthony Fauci, to be sure; but neither are you or I: he was a seafarer and an explorer. Ergo, there was nothing genocidal about it. The genocide narrative may suit "woke" people and political organizers, so-called "educated" and trained Marxist-Leninist movements like the BLM, with their white wannabe followers who feel ashamed for their race and feel compelled to help set a "level playing field" to correct their apparent "white privilege," but they really know not what they do, – and it does not square with reality or history. The more scientific, knowledgeable, or exact amongst us know differently.

None of which stops people from pulling down Columbus' statues if they want to – like Mike Forcia and other Native American activists in St. Paul, Minnesota did last year.[2] I suppose the waves of 19th-century Italian immigrants who saw in Columbus, rightly, a man to be proud of, had a different story to tell about racism than today's downtrodden people who seem, overall, and compared to the past, to be doing quite fine these days. It could be instructive for them to see how the Italians turned something negative into a positive: how they created something from their adversity, without destroying anything in its place.

Like all great men, Columbus is a complicated man with a complicated story.

In a Bloyian universe, it may not really matter. Because, for Bloy, all events in history are symbolic and must be seen from the lens of a divine will to truly understand and appreciate them. This book, Part One of *The Revealer of the Globe,* is similar in style

---

[2]Mike Forcia: he has apparently been charged for the act of vandalism, and so should he be.

to a later work written by Bloy, *The Soul of Napoleon*,[3] of which see. In both books' forewords is a discussion of the pulling down of statues by partisans of people of color. In the foreword to *The Soul of Napoleon,* a rather lengthy footnote explained in greater detail the charge of "hypocrisy and self-serving claptrap" made against the BLM:

> *Witness whereof the news item that broke just days after this foreword was first written, reporting that BLM co-founder, Patrisse Cullors, had recently bought a $1,400,000 home in an affluent "white" neighborhood of Topanga Canyon (the Hollywood Hills basically) in Los Angeles, California... One has to wonder whether Ms. Cullors, originally from Pacoima, and a self-professed "trained Marxist," is still in favor of defunding the police now that she has purchased her new homes (yes homes, she owns more than four in the U.S. and several outside the U.S.);... Also, a $1.4 million home and "four high-end houses for $3.2 million in the US alone, according to property records" according to a New York Post article (April 10, 2021) is a lot of capitalism and private property for someone who "spent years absorbing*

[3]*The Soul of Napoleon*: also available in English by Sunny Lou Publishing.

Marxist-Leninist ideology."[4]

Similar in hypocrisy and claptrap are some indigenous peoples of America – I don't say all, because
that would be racist, but the few, or more than a few
perhaps, – who accuse Columbus of "genocide,"
knowing full well, I trust, that death by smallpox is
not genocide, which involves intention, and cannot be

---

[4]Since then, Ms. Cullors has announced, on May 27, 2021, that
she will step down as "executive director" of the BLM
organization which she helped found. She declared, according to
a *U.S. Today* article on May 28, that she had been planning to do
so for more than a year prior, and that her decision has nothing
to do with the recent leak of her financial situation. "Those were
right-wing attacks that tried to discredit my character, and I don't
operate off of what the right thinks about me," she is reported to
have said.

Everyone is free to believe her words and actions at
face value if they wish to. One assumes she plans to keep the
3.4 million worth of real-estate. How many properties can one
Marxist-Leninist person inhabit at the same time? Of course, she
never said she subscribed to Locke's theories of property that I
remember. Rather than keep all her wealth and step down, she
could have chosen another way to react to the news leak: for one
thing, she could have admitted how bad it looked, sold a property
or two, and donated money to black institutions to help educate
or support other black people less fortunate than herself. Isn't
that what the BLM is all about – or is it merely about overthrowing
the current form of U.S. government, doing away with the family,
shaming white people, practicing iconoclasm, filling all important
positions of power with black people, etc.?

Of course, the two candidates to replace her are also
black and women (by birth one assumes, but it is harder and
harder to tell these days). One cannot trust a white person, or a
male, let alone a white male, in such a role. But white people are
supposed to trust black people in all sorts of other roles, –
otherwise we would be racist. Seems fair and unbiased to me.

charged against Columbus. Pulling down a statue is a much more clear-cut offense.

Same goes for the kind, intoxicated, somewhat in-my-face indigenous man at the bus depot in Anchorage who was appalled that I, a white man, should support white people. For when he said "white people," what he really meant was "bad people."

It is the same narrative, gaining traction since the 1960s, by the same groups of people who are unable to be, or who feel unable to become, great themselves, – no matter how many opportunities they have or have had to lift themselves up – and who insist instead to feel sorry for themselves – for decades and centuries on end, – always asking for reparations from contemporary people who had no hand in their past situations. Their only conception of achieving something great is to defecate or vomit on the statues of prior great white men, assuming any statues remain standing. Is it still taught in public school and textbooks that the United States waged a civil war, an internecine war against itself, in part to end slavery? Does anyone hear the BLM or people of color talking about that, showing their gratitude to the many white people who gave their lives for an idea? Were there any organized displays of remembrance and gratitude on Memorial Day for the fallen, white Civil War soldiers?

No man, great or otherwise, is perfect – except Jesus Christ maybe, but even he was complicated and not always consistent, based on what we understand of him and his life from the first four Gospels of the New Testament. He too had something to be upset about: his crucifixion. Instead, he's got only love for his oppressors. But I have yet to hear a single word from the angry and ungrateful masses today, – so anti-white and anti-Western Civilization – as to what they plan to erect in place of all the statues and memorials to the thousands of great white men they have knocked down or plan to, and whose benefits to humanity they share in.

Unless they be statues to victims.[5] Which, frankly, are statues symbolic of hatred, intended to shame a certain group of people holistically for the bad acts of a few, and are not statues symbolic of past glory or greatness, intended to inspire everyone. They have nothing to do with creating something new and positive of one's own, but everything to do with destroying, denigrating, and negating another race and people. The only new thing that the BLM proposes, fundamentally, today, is that white people voluntarily concede power and position, and switch roles with them. White people deserve what they get if they accept the gambit. It will solve none of the current ills in the West today. It will likely make them worse. But it may be the first time – in the history of the world – that one race of people willfully considered going into servitude at the request of another, and for shame.

– Richard Robinson, Anchorage, Memorial Day, 2021

---

[5]statues to victims. For more on this, and a proposal to end some of the Western world's current ills, see Dr. Helmut Schleppend's *An Immodest Proposal*, by Sunny Lou Publishing.

Declaration by the Author

In my capacity as a Catholic, I declare to submit entirely to the Church's doctrine, to the rules and decisions of the Holy See, notably to the Decrees of Sovereign Pontiffs Urban VIII and Benedict XIV, concerning the canonization of Saints.

      If I should happen, on the subject of the present Cause for Beatification, to employ the words "Saint" or "Sanctity," it is merely in a purely relative way, for insufficiency of language, for lack of terms that might render my thought more completely. In advance, I disavow the rigorous and absolute meaning that one would attribute to those expressions; for no one can be called a SAINT as long as the Church has not officially qualified him as such.

      LÉON BLOY

      PARIS, 12 JULY 1883.

Preface

The author of the preface you are now reading was one of the first to speak about that beautiful book of history – cause and occasion of this other book that is published today.[6]

It was in 1856. A man, at that time, took note one day of the monstruosity under which the world lived in peace and went about its business. The fact of the matter was that Christopher Columbus, – one of the greatest men who ever existed, if not the greatest, – literally had no history. Transported by shame on behalf of the human race, that man, who was a writer of the most elevated talent, resolved to lift up, as best he could, Christopher Columbus out of the destiny of silence and ingratitude that weighed down on his memory for nearly four centuries, and which had made the greatness of oblivion proportionate to the greatness of the service rendered by him to the entire world. Until then, meager notes, deceptive or derisory, scribbled about Christopher Columbus had shown that they were worthy of the hands that had crossed out his name in order to replace it with another's as regards the great discovery[7]... and, for the first time, with the publication in 1856, the life of Christopher Columbus was written.

Unfortunately, the marble of oblivion is harder to scratch than the marble of a tomb, and it has to

[6] Original footnote: Les Œuvres et les hommes, 2nd vol., The Historians.

[7] to replace it with another's: Amerigo Vespucci's.

be said that the *History of Christopher Columbus*, by the Count Roselly de Lorgues, in spite of all the good one might have to say about it, had not at all, at a time when publicity is prostituted on the lowest of literary works, the resounding success that men take for glory. But here is a book that will avenge the book that has too long remained in the dark! Let's see where the seed of truth cast into the slight and imbecilic winds fell!

It fell into the heart of the Pope who governed the Church at that time, and all of a sudden it took root and grew!... In the immensely great man who was Christopher Columbus, Pius IX saw the saint that needed to come out, – and by his pontifical hand, with that hand that arranges eternity, he prepared an altar for him. From that moment on, the Beatification of Christopher Columbus was resolved upon... In order to be one with the latent intuition of the mystical heart of Pius IX, the Count Roselly de Lorgues was solemnly appointed, in Roman chancellery style, "the Postulator of the Cause before the Sacred Congregation of Rites." What glory! the missing glory, late in coming but finally come and not from below whence it often comes, but from on high whence it ought always to originate. In spite of everything, in effect, in spite of the contagion of Freethinking, that terrible modern cholera of Freethinking[8] that gnaws at them and diminishes them with each passing day, Chris-

---

[8]Freethinking: for more about Freemasonry and the Catholic Church, see "Leo XIII and the Conspiration of Imbeciles" in Bloy's *Words of a Demolitions Contractor*, Sunny Lou Publishing.

tians are still numerous enough to achieve glory, as the world conceives it and wants it – and, by the very fact that the Church made inquiries into the sanctity of Christopher Columbus, he had his glory, even in the eyes of the Church's enemies, who, fundamentally, know quite well, in what remains of the soul they possess, that there is nothing on earth comparable in glory to that!

And at the same time, the Count Roselly de Lorgues had his glory also. He had too indissolubly attached his noble life to the colossal life of Christopher Columbus for it to be possibly detached from it. From then on, whoever thought of the hero thought by consequence of the historian who had recounted his life. The Count Roselly de Lorgues has written his name so deeply into the name of Christopher Columbus that one cannot read the one without seeing the other, in the light that the Church sheds on them, with its torch. Christopher Columbus and Roselly de Lorgues will be allotted, each at his own level, a share of the same immortality...

Of course, it is not for such men that I write this preface. They have no need for it. They are high above every living quill. If prefaces signify anything, it is when they are previsions of the Criticism in favor of Obscure men whom it draws out from their obscurity and whom it must enjoy bringing into the light. Like M. Léon Bloy and his book on *THE REVEALER OF THE GLOBE* that the Count Roselly de Lorgues' history and his devotion to the memory of Columbus had inspired.

Now, M. Léon Bloy is precisely one of those obscure men that Criticism has a duty to push to the stars, provided they have the strength to climb. Admirer and servant of Christopher Columbus and the Count Roselly de Lorgues, M. Léon Bloy was not content merely to point out the sublimities of his history, as written by Count Roselly. He did not write a book on a book merely, as all criticism has the right to do or arrogate. He did better and greater than that. By speaking of the *only* historian of Christopher Columbus, he has become the latter's historian as well, in his own manner and the second after the first! He did not place his foot servilely in the luminous rut of a subject where a great talent's chariot of fire had already passed! But he thought on the subject, in his own and private fashion, with a novel depth and energy. *The History of Christopher Columbus* by the Count Roselly de Lorgues had suggested a book to M. Léon Bloy, but it did not diminish the originality of his own work. It had, on the contrary, fecundated it. It was the springboard from which that robust mind launched itself to a height that will astonish those certainly who are not capable of such bounds. Now that the Church has seized on it, no one can touch, in order to improve on it, a *Catholic* glory that is on the verge of perfection. I will not add then one iota to that glory with my iota of a preface. I prefer to leave it to M. Léon Bloy, and may that iota be the first spark that shines on a talent, today as yet unknown, but which, tomorrow perhaps, will set everything on fire!

For it is a spirit on fire, composed of faith and enthusiasm, is that unknown Léon Bloy, who cannot stay unknown for long once his book is published... For my part, among Catholic writers of the present hour, I do not know anyone of that ardor, of that violence of love, of that fanaticism for the truth. It is even that incompressible fanaticism, which he boasts of as his best faculty, that has prevented M. Léon Bloy from proving in the eyes of the world his other faculties and his superiority as a writer. Polemicist by temperament, made for every fight, every combat, and feeling that vocation for war boiling inside him, as that sort of vocation boils in souls, when there is one, he early on asked instantly of those who seemed to think like him for a place on their battlefields, but they always shut the entrance to their camp on him.

Is that surprising? In an epoch when the genius of the Concession that governs the world goes so far as to let everything run loose, a soul of that absoluteness and rigor frightened those even whom he would have best served. The heroic Veuillot, for example, who never trembled before anything, except before talents that would have considered it an honor to fight beside him for the cause of the Church, Veuillot grew afraid, one day, of M. Léon Bloy's talent, and, after four or five articles accepted by him in *l'Univers*, he let him go formally.[9] At that time, that man, with whom one conducted oneself as if he was a young man, when he was a grown man, and who, for ten years, was waiting and growing impatient, accumulating and amassing within himself the strength to become the most

---

[9]Veuillot... let him go finally: see *The Desperate Man*.

formidable of journalists, was suffocated by the cowardly strength of the journals' silence, and the journals on which he ought to have counted most! Thrown, like the prophet Daniel, into the pit of beasts, but with beasts that were not lions, he began again to do what he has always done his whole life. He began again to wait, with the weight of his talent, which was misunderstood and which weighed down on his heart, for the favorable occasion when he could prove his mettle, to his friends and his enemies. And that dazzling occasion was the Beatification of Christopher Columbus, in which he has demonstrated, against the vile quibblers of that great measure *put forward by Pius IX*, the omnipotence of blows that he could deal them and that others recognized in him, but also another omnipotence that was not recognized!

And it is the unexpected omnipotence that comes from somewhere deeper than in the soul or in the genius of the man and which hovers above all literature. That extraordinary omnipotence has gushed out of M. Léon Bloy from the depths of his faith. Without his absolute faith in the supernaturalness of the Church, he would not have written about Him who is called "the Revealer of the Globe," a story as supernatural as the Church itself, and he would not have blended them, the one and the other, into so sublime an identification. M. Léon Bloy's book, that the Church's enemies will accuse of mysticism so as to insult him and so as not to respond to it, as if Mysticism were not the last glimmer that God might permit a man to light a fire with in the hearth of his Love so as to penetrate the mystery of his Providence; this book, having dug deeper into the history than the Count Roselly de Lorgues had, into the entrails of divine reality, is even more a glorification of the Church than a glorification of Christopher Columbus. Separate, in fact, in your mind, the personality of Christopher Columbus from the synthesis of the world that, alone, the Church embraces and that, alone, it explains, and you will see only one man anymore at that scale of human greatness; but, with the Church, and forming one body with it, he becomes immediately the great providential man, the visible and fleshly arm of God, anticipated at the origin of the world by the prophets of early on... The reasons for that miraculous situation in the economy of creation, irrefragable for all Christians who do not wish to fall into the abyss of inconsequence, cannot, I know, be accepted by minds that chase away at this time, systematically, God from everywhere; but the expression of truth, which they take for an error, is so great here that they will be forced to admire him.

That dogmatic part of M. Léon Bloy's book is really *sacred history*, as Pascal's genius even would have been able to conceive it or write about it had he thought to consider the life of Christopher Columbus, and to explain that prodigious intervention in human things, of that Revealer of the Globe who could be called, after the Divine Redeemer, the second redeemer of humanity!

I can think of nobody else really besides the author of *Pensées* to treat of such a lofty subject, forgotten by Bossuet, with that super-acute apperception of seeing things, that strength to conceive things in their entirety, that depth of interpretation, and that majesty of language, with its Biblical savors. I want above all to insist on this point. M. Léon Bloy, – the writer without an audience until now, and whose several friends alone know the eloquent violence that will be found again, for all that, in the third part of his book, when he descends from the heights found at the beginning of his apologetics, – M. Léon Bloy has taken from the Holy Books in which he has steeped himself for so long, the entire reach of his thought, the placidity of his strength, and the temperance of his sagacity; and the style of that great man *calmed* by the Holy Spirit is no longer the style *that is the man*, as Buffon said.[10]

It is not in the limited space of a simple preface that one can cite anything from that exuberant book of continuous beauty, which must be taken in the vast plenitude of its unity in order to judge it. This preface, which says nothing because the book that follows it says everything, is nothing but a pointer to the book that must be brought to others' attention so that they might notice it. It has nothing more to say than the few words of the mysterious voice that spoke to Saint Augustine, under the fig tree: "*Take this and read.*" Augustine read, and we know what followed.

Will the men of this period read that book, which is too heavy for their feeble hands and feeble minds?...

[10]Buffon: Georges-Louis Leclerc (AD 1707-1788), count de Buffon, in his *Discourse on style*.

Only, after they have read it, when they return to reading the books of this epoch's puerile and sottish trinketry, will they have the sensation of a universal watering down that wants to make us vanish into emptiness, that paradise of imbeciles?... And there is always that at least, for the benefit and for the glory of truth.

– J. Barbey d'Aurevilly

Part One: Exposé and Historical Background of the Cause

"Spiritus sanctus corporali specie sicut COLUMBA." –
LUKE, 3:22

I

For many years now, in the world, the project to beatify Christopher Columbus has been talked about. That extraordinary project, suggestive of grandiose thoughts, did not produce at first those immense outflows of popularity among Christians that it seemed humanly reasonable to expect. Universal enthusiasm did not break out. Some journals perpetually hostile to Christianity pointed out, in passing, that new "encroachment" of ultramontane clericalism, some with a disdain full of good-naturedness, others with a sort of contained rage. Freethinking has the originality to suppose that the Church is stealing something from it when It permits itself to canonize the saints. The Pride of men believes that they, alone, have the right to place someone on their own altars. But Catholic journals, not having believed they needed to give to a simple project that was of a realization then both distant and uncertain, the resounding publicity of a near and ineluctable event, the fierce dissatisfaction of our enemies flagged all on its own, and the public did not even notice something great had been in question.

Today, that forgotten affair returns with more strength than ever and begins to take shape like the ardent preoccupation of a great number of religious souls a little bit everywhere. That movement, having originated in France, merits, surely, to be studied, and that is the object of this work. It appeared necessary, before the purely hagiographic matter should be taken up by whomever it may concern, to present here some historical and biographical considerations that will allow the multitude of Christians to grasp at one and the same time its importance and opportunity.

If M. the Count Roselly de Lorgues, the Catholic historian of Christopher Columbus and the official Postulator of his Cause before the Holy Congregation of Rites, was able to be intoxicated on that heady deception that is called human glory, he could, from today forward, rest and go to sleep in the security and perfect plentitude of triumph. For he has made a thing by which his name will be perpetually contemporary with one of the most immortal preoccupations of humanity. He has given himself the imperishable glory of being the revealer of Him by whom the totality of Creation was revealed to us. Before him, nobody really knew Christopher Columbus, and the universal ignorance was more wide-spread than the knowledge of it had made believe, as the prejudice of calumny had become unwavering and consistent like an axiom.

That majestic personality of the Discoverer of the New World passed into history like a scientific illustration of average grandeur that the nearness of Bernard de Palissy or Benjamin Franklin did not detract from. The discovery of half the Earth had become, after three hundred years, something of an instructive anecdote in the popular manuals of science for everyone and in the historico-literary *recreations* of the endearing *Practical Morality*. The universitarian and imperturbable synopses mentioned simply that once upon a time, on such and such a date, *a Genoese pilot* who sought one knows not what, discovered, *by chance*, America, and that was it. The Dragon of modern childishness had opened its paper gob over the most enormous event in history and had irremediably swallowed it. But it happened that, one fine day, that event tore up his ridiculous insides and was thrown up into the sky in one shot. Mysterious Providence, which does not know haste and for which it is never *too late*, had left all its obscure and squatting blasphemers to crawl and slaver for nearly four centuries over the memory of its Messenger.

When the moment fixed by It and known by It alone had arrived, nothing august remained anymore under the belly of reptiles, and the Servant of Jesus Christ extended his miraculous hands over the most noble faces, and the apotheosis began.

The great Pope Pius IX, the first, the *only* of all Roman Pontiffs who had visited the New World, deeply struck by Christopher Columbus' providential role and magnificently impatient for the man's glory, whose *sanctity* he felt, by virtue of his infallible sagacity as Supreme Pastor, ordered, soon after his return from Gaeta, that the history of the Christian navigator, to whom we owe America, recounted until that time exclusively by Protestant quills, should be finally written in its entirety by a Catholic and presented in its true aspect.

As the oldest Daughter of the Church had led opinion astray and given the name of a plagiarist to the Continent discovered by God's Envoy,[11] it was France itself whom the Head of the Church charged with repairing, as much as possible, that injustice, by publishing in its language the life of that sublime apostle. The Holy Father selected, for that work, from among French Catholic writers, the last representative of a race recommendable for centuries by its hereditary devotion to the Papacy, M. the Count Roselly de Lorgues, present dean of our Catholic writers.[12] He did not confide it to a sacerdotal quill because that biography is not purely historical or religious, but because it consists of very diverse appreciations, touches on multiple interests, and concerns the entire world without acceptation of belief or governments.

At the back of Pius IX's thought was that this

------

[11]name of a plagiarist: Amerigo Vespucci.

[12]Original footnote: a Brief from April 24, 1863, mentions the Italian origin of the Count Roselly de Lorgues and the ancient illustriousness of his race. In 1309, the Chevalier Jean Roselli accompanied to Avignon the Pope Clement V who came to set himself up there.

The Count Antoine Roselli, although laic, was Legate of the Holy See five times, for Popes Martin V and Eugene IV. His cousin Jean-Baptiste, a simple abbot, held the same honor twice. Successively, other Roselli served the Papacy directly: also, by naming the Count Roselly de Lorgues Commander of the Order, the great Pius IX was pleased to recall the services of his ancestors and their loyalty to the Holy See. (Brief from July 3, 1866.)

publicity would revive public attention, prepare Christian spirits for an august approval, and finally provoke some imposing Catholic manifestation in the sense of the great act of justice that he was pondering. M. the Count Roselly de Lorgues published then, in 1856, for the first time, the magnificent *History of the Life and Voyages of Christopher Columbus*. That restitution, equivalent to a discovery, deeply surprised opinion and earned for its author the incomparable satisfaction of being insulted by the greater part of the Church's enemies. For nearly thirty years, the *History of Christopher Columbus* had to submit to the fate providentially reserved for all transcendent productions of the spirit of faith, above all at that time. It quietly awaits the hour of its great brilliance, insinuating itself little by little and slowly into some superior souls who might find it in front of them without having sought for it, and who, having found it, can no longer forget it.

That book, one of the finest historic efforts of this century of historians, was, for some of those souls that whinny at the sublime and whom the world's pasturages do not satisfy, like a supererogatory revelation added to the other Revelation. After so many famous exegeses emanated from so many golden Mouths, that profound recitation of the adventures of a man of God had the effect of a new commentary on the Holy Book, of the most unexpected kind, written for the first time by an inspired hand, in the tangible clarity of history.

The world was already familiar with that great sort of interpretation of the divine Word experimentally confronted by human events. There was the *City of God* by Saint Augustine, and the glorious *Discourse on Universal History*.[13] A writer of almost supernatural genius, Joseph de Maistre, Angelic Doctor of Providential Dogma, from the extremity of his quill dipped in light, had shown some of the visible laws of the temporal government of God on peoples and on empires. But what had never been seen before, since the Gospels, was the confused Babel of all the prophetic testimonies, contradictorily human and divine, in every century, coming to pile up and accumulate, like a mountain of Transfiguration, under the feet of a single man predestined for the gigantesque misfortune of having to consume them.

And that unique man, about whom it is nearly impossible to speak without trembling, when one knows what God had placed in him and what other men had done to him, it is Christopher Columbus – the mysterious *Dove*[14] *carrying the Christ*! – manifestly charged with rendering possible, by perpetual and *universal* oblation of the Holy Sacrifice,[15] the most profoundly obscure prophecies of the Old Testament. And there you have it, what the book by the Count Roselly de Lorgues dared to bring out for the first time in a recitation of such palpitation and so ten-

---

[13]*Discourse on Universal History*: by Jacques-Benigne Bossuet (AD 1627-1704), published in 1681.

[14]Dove: Christopher Columbus in French is *Christophe Colomb*, which etymologically could be construed to mean Christ-carrying Dove.

[15]Holy Sacrifice: the Holy Sacrifice of the Mass: i.e., the Eucharist.

der a pity for that poor giant of the apostolate crushed under the Cross that he carries to half of humanity; in the reading of which, souls melt with compassion, and about which one is tempted to ask amorously of the Lord, – in view of what dreadful claims on His justice does He permit the ingratitude of men to exert themselves to such an extent on the most generous friends of His glory!?

II

Of all the things that time exterminates or dishonors, nothing is more fragile, more effaceable, than aston-ishment. At the distance of four centuries, what poet's imagination would be capable of conceiving of the in-expressible stupefaction of the old Christian world, not yet contaminated by the snout of the Reformation, on the news of the discovery of an unknown world that Christ and his Apostles had not spoken about? That fifteenth-century society, – built, like Babylon, impregnable from the Almighty, guarded by the sa-cred double wall of Theology and Tradition, and gird-ed by a mystical ditch wherein the blood of several millions of martyrs boiled, – must have been sur-prised, in so vehement a manner, that it would be puerile to seek in history another example of such prodigious disconcertment.

The haughty intelligences of that time must have feared that the Church itself was going to go to ruin with its triple diadem and its indefectible prom-ises. The Mission exposed by Christopher Columbus humiliated, on several essential points, the scholastic despotism of an inflexible exegesis wherein the Letter of the Holy Books suffocated the Spirit of the Lord.[16] Catholic Science, stuck on formulas and sentences from School, had ended up by sterilizing Tradition, by turning it away from contemplation of divine objects in order to constrain it to explain *everything* in the political order and in the subjective order of natural realities.

Imperturbable and serene, that science clutched onto the human race and spread itself out before God's Wisdom, like a shore before the Ocean, so that that Wisdom "might not go any further" and condescended to break, against the granite of syllogism, "the swelling of its waves."

----

[16]Original footnote: When Columbus, in instance to the Court of Spain, had to appear before the Junta of Salamanca charged with the examination of his project of Discovery, several learned members of that congress "objected to his deductions using passages from Holy Scriptures which they applied extremely poorly and fragments taken from several ecclesiastical authors contrary to his system. *Cathedratic* professors established by major and minor argument that the Earth is flat like a rug, and could not be round, given the Psalmist spoke of: 'Stretching the earth *like a hide*,' *extendens cœlum sicut pellem*; which would be impossible to do if it were spherical. They opposed him with the words of Saint Paul, comparing the skies to a tent deployed above the Earth, which excluded the rotundity of this world. Others, less rigid, or less strangers to cosmography, sustained, that by admitting that the Earth was round, the project of going in search of regions inhabited in the austral hemisphere was chimerical, given that the other half of the world was occupied by the TENEBROUS SEA, that formidable and unlimited gulf; and if, by good fortune, a ship launched in that direction succeeded in reaching India, news of it would never get back to them, because that pretended rotundity of the Earth would form an insurmountable obstacle to his return, however favorable one might suppose the winds." (*Christopher Columbus*, by the Count Roselly de Lorgues, book I, chapter V.)

The sudden appearance of a Messenger and of a Revealer in the midst of a society so firmly set in the certitude that all divine revelations were consummated was, without a doubt, for a large number of lofty minds, a formidable proof preliminary to the tempestuous Lutheran expugnment. One is forced to recognize it, – the two simultaneous events of the Discovery of the New World and the Renaissance of the Ancient World were of such a nature to disconcert human reason and to make the universitarian milk of the most orthodox doctrines turn sour.

Naïve souls, to be honest, found it very simple that God might not have revealed everything to the docents and that he should wish to make some new things. They judged that, after all, there was no reason to despair of his Wisdom just because it did not docilely align with the philosophical exigencies of his creation. Those souls were the clairvoyants and the unwavering folk of the most dislocated century in history, and it is for them above all that Christopher Columbus declared with the boldness of a transcendent simplicity that God had made him "Messenger of a new earth and new skies." "The Lord," he added, "listens sometimes to the prayers of servants who follow his precepts, even in things that appear impossible and that intelligence cannot conceive of nor attain."

One thing, among others, that human intelligence would not know how to grapple with, with the frightening foreshortening of its notion of justice, is the mystery of an entire half of the human race excluded, for more than five thousand years, from all participation in the spiritual life of peoples of the Ancient World. That simple fact blows one's mind!

What nameless, measureless crime was able then to necessitate so long and so dreadful an expiation, endured, not by a single people, but by hundreds of nations, for some of whom it continues still? What am I saying? The greater part of them did not see any light rise, and the aurora of oriental civilization was for the multitude of those unfortunate creatures like the announcement of a deluge of blood and fire over the waves of the Atlantic.

That unknown terrestrial hemisphere – like that mysterious half of the moon perpetually inobservable, – rolled through space with the rest of the world for two million days. In vain the Candelabra of the Revelation had been promenaded from Orient to Occident. Ever since Abraham, extending under the feet of the future Messiah – like a miraculous Milky Way of human hearts – all his *stellar* posterity, for twenty-two centuries; and, from Jesus, vanquisher of Death, to Mahomet, vanquisher of Byzantium, innumerable generations, obscure and luminous, had soaked the earth with their tears, with their sweat, or with their blood. Powerful civilizations had extended their influences in all directions of the human spirit. Miraculous intelligences had exhausted every conjecture. Saints, martyrs, apostles even to whom the Savior had spoken with his mouth to teach all nations, had accomplished their mandate over only half the globe, abandoning the other half in an invincible ignorance of the Redemption. The most audacious, the most indefatigable of the Twelve, privileged Witness of the Son of God's Resurrection, – he who is, said Saint Bridget, God's treasure and the light of the world, – Doubting Thomas, leaving Alexander the Great among other dust in his path behind him, had advanced as far as the extreme banks of the Orient. There, feeling perhaps, before dying, the mute and distant clamor of those abandoned souls, he had need-lessly extended his arms of an apostle above that in-commensurable Pacific Ocean, moving and deceptive barrier that mocked his desire...

Nothing divine and nothing human had been able to prevail against the inexorable *darknesses* of those inexplicably chastised races!

III

Now I ask permission to speak of the Devil.

The *worldly sort*, generally persuaded of the inexistence of the *Prince of this world* and for whom this labor is principally destined, will forgive me per-haps for this digression necessary for an understand-ing of the mission, Catholically envisaged, of Christo-pher Columbus.

The notion of the Devil is, of all modern things, that which lacks the most depth, by dint of having become literary. Assuredly, the Demon of the majority of poets would not frighten children even. I know of only a single poetic Satan who is really terri-ble. It is Baudelaire's, *because he is* SACRILEGIOUS. All others', including Dante's, leave our souls quite tranquil and their menaces would make little girls of

the catechism of perseverance shrug their very unlit-
erary shoulders. But the real Satan that one no longer
knows, the Satan of Theology and of the Mystic
Saints, – the Antagonist of Woman and the Tempter
of Jesus Christ, – that one there is so monstrous that,
if the Slave were allowed to show himself such as he
is – in the supernatural nakedness of Non-Love, – the
human race and the animal world altogether would
simply let out a cry and die...

Satan's greatest strength is his *Irrevocability*.
The word "fatalism," invented by the so-called philosophical pride of men, is nothing but an obscure
translation of that terrifying attribute of the Prince of
Evil Men and the Emperor of Captives. God keeps for
himself his Providence, his Justice, his Mercy, and,
above all else, the *Right of Grace* which is like a seal
on which his omnipotent Sovereignty is imprinted. He
also keeps the Irrevocability of Joy and he leaves to
Satan the irrevocability of Despair. The terrifying
pale door of the great American poet[17] is open above
those two gulfs offered to our freedom of choice.

Now, irrevocability begins with this life. It is
formulated in a free act and is accomplished by perseverance. Grace intervenes merely to prevent freedom
from slipping out of our soul and from being lost in
the terrifying anguish of Temptation. But Irrevocability subsists in facts, in so redoubtable a manner, that
the least whims, the least thoughts, the most fugitive
palpitations have infinite consequences and echo forever. Here, everything is magnified. Contingency

---

[17]*pale door*... American poet: most likely a reference to Edgar
Allen Poe and his poem, "The Fall of the House of Usher."

does not pass over the sill of moral life, and a free being's moral life, contained within the inflexible limits of its personality, does not go and lose itself in contingency. One must *absolutely* be wholly prey to either eternal joy or eternal despair.

When the Demon seduces and gets the better of our freedom, he obtains thereby the terrible children of our race and his race, immortal like their father or mother. That progeniture bears children and pullulates in turn, indefinitely, without any *natural* means given to us that we might stop that horrible and incalculable multiplication of witnesses to our dishonor.

It is the illimitable empire of Satan. He reigns as a patriarch over the multitude of awful children of human freedom. He adopts them all as soon as they are born. His ministers, his officers, his chamberlains, and his majordomos take care of them. It is an army against each of us, an immense army of invasion that outflanks our souls at every instant, at the hour of action as at the hour of repose, at the hour of joy as at the hour of sadness, at the hour of sleep and of dream, at the hour even of prayer and of the most saintly effusions of the heart, but above all at the definitive and troubling hour of death. That pitiless war without truce has for a signal the dictate of our will alone, dictate without appeal, irrevocable promulgation, sanctioned by infallible Justice. God may pardon and pardons in fact; but evil is nonetheless accomplished for eternity and does not stop, over the course of time, to produce terrifying fruits that the Demon places continually in front of our eyes so as to make us despair.

I repeat, that there is his strength; that there is his portion, his *majorat* as the Prince of lies and the poisoned flower of his special punishment! He girds the earth with his two immense arms like a scarf of mourning and of death, like the *mare Tenebrosum*[18] in the cosmography of the ancients. Nothing escapes his grip, nothing... except the crucified freedom of Jesus Christ. Outside of calvary, he is master of everything, and one can stick a label on him with the name of every nefarious influence in life. He is on everyone's lips, and everyone toasts to him; he is seated at every celebration, and he satisfies our hunger for horrors amidst triumphs; he is lying in the darkest corner of the nuptial bed; he gnaws on and sullies all our feelings, all our hopes, all our purities, all our virginities, and all our glories! His preferred throne is the golden chalice of love in bloom, and his sweetest bath is the purple foyer of love in flames. When we are not speaking of God or for God, it is the Devil that we are speaking of or listening to... in a formidable silence. He empoisons the rivers of life and the fountainheads of death, he digs precipices in the middle of our paths, he arms all nature against us, to the point that God has had to confide the protection of each of us to a celestial spirit so that we might not perish from the very instant of our birth. Finally, Satan is seated atop the earth, with his feet on the five parts of the world and nothing *human* is accomplished without him intervening, without him having intervened, and without him needing to intervene. There is nothing to be surprised by in that enormous power of his, and Catholic reason is not surprised by it. Satan has nothing but what God

---

[18]*mare Tenebrosum*: Latin for "Tenebrous Sea."

gives him, and God gives him everything... with the exception of human freedom.

IV

Imagine for yourself now that immense American continent, extending from one pole to the other for nearly four thousand leagues, so immeasurable in all ways that it would have taken several Romes to conquer only its littoral, and that after three hundred ninety years the most audacious scientific explorations have been unable to know it in its entirety.

That interminable chain of peoples, strangers amongst themselves, and of diverse languages, separated by all the differences of mores and climate, divided by hereditary hatreds and by religions whose perfect atrocities were their sole unity: such was at the moment of Discovery the exclusive apanage of the Spirit of evil!

Without a doubt, the rest of the earth belonged to that monarch, in the manner I have just mentioned; but, here, he was the absolute master, legislator, father, and God. There was no Redeemer or Gospel to fear. The Blood of Jesus Christ clearly would not flow across the Ocean. The true God seemed to have abdicated all suzerainty over that unfortunate world, having left it apparently, without any relief, for a number of centuries equal to the number of years that make up an old man.

"You are the children of the Devil," said Jesus Christ to the Jews who prided themselves for having

God as their father. That affirmation, so mysterious and clearly terrible at the same time, coming from such a mouth, did not apply only to that infidel and dissolute nation. It passed well beyond and went far and away to attain, through the figurative race, all races and all prevaricative human families, to the last extremities of space and time. But how real, how frightening, how more mysterious still that sentence must have appeared if one comes to consider the total abandonment, the absolute exile of those multitudes in his image that the living God seemed to have separated forever and who did not resemble the multitude of witnesses of the Lamb who are spoken about in the Apocalypse except in the impossibility of counting them!

A great, modern philosopher has said that ancient slavery was for gentiles an entirely virtual and internal Christianity.[19] Assuredly, the forty centuries of slavery preceding evangelical diffusion must have weighed down heavily on the heart of man; but when all is said and done, the darkness of Paganism, as thick as it was, was not an absolute darkness. Edenic Revelation had left profound imprints in the reasonable clay. Primitive historians, rhapsodes, old tragedians are saturated with divine and prophetic supernaturalism. Sublime flashes of light traversed sometimes that chaos and came to illuminate the simulacra and altars with strange symbolic shimmers. The great Promise voyaged in the world among generations of involuntary penitents and, from age to age, was formulated obscurely, in the manner of a distant echo, in

---

[19]Original footnote: Saint Bonnet, *la Douleur*.

the inspired clamor of Sibylline voices. Legislations themselves, so proud and so strict, had let themselves be penetrated as if by a vague presentiment of human dignity. The Demon triumphed clearly, but with inquietude, and he trembled before his slaves!...

In America, nothing of the sort. Absolute darkness and complete triumph, as in hell! The book of Wisdom has a passage, sublime with horror, wherein King Solomon recounts the miraculous *blindness* of Egypt, region of *anguish*, figurative of all paganism:

"They were all there together," said the royal Seer, "bound by the same chain of darkness and enveloped by one long night. Enclosed under their roofs, they had gone to bed, fugitives of perpetual Providence.

"And, imagining to themselves that they could remain hidden in the obscurity of their sins, they had been dispersed under an obscure veil of oblivion, – being horribly frightened and trembling prodigiously.

"For the cavern that contained them did not protect them from fear, because every sound that came down to them filled them with fright...

"The whistling of the wind; the sweet song of birds in the tree branches; the sound of running water; that of rocks falling; the gambols, invisible to them, of animals; the howlings of wild beasts or the resounding echoes from mountain hollows: all those things made them die for fright...

"There was no fire of any strength that could

give them any light, and the limpid flames of stars could not shine a light on that horrible night...

"It is then that the prestige of magic art appeared derisory and that glorious wisdom was ridiculed with ignominy.

"Because those who promised to banish all fear and all perturbations of the languishing soul, languished themselves, ridiculously, full of terrors...

"They were all sleeping the same sleep in that night of powerlessness that came to them *from the deepest of hells*...

"Now, all the rest of the world was illuminated by a brilliant light and accomplished its works, without any hindrance.

"They alone were crushed down by the heavy night, image of darkness that had to appear to them. And they had become more unbearable to themselves than their own darkness."[20]

They were alone! What a terrifying destiny! and what a master to stand in for God! A *chain of darkness* for all theology and supreme, perpetual terror for every legislation! From north to south, one could walk an entire Indian life and four thousand leagues without encountering Hope. That marvelous nature that ravished the *Conquistadores*, – to the point of making one think for an instant of Christopher Columbus whom the terrible Cherub no longer stood sentinel for, with his sword of fire, and whom Christ's children were finally going to cover again

_____
[20]Original footnote: See chap. XVII.

with a Paradise Lost, – the newcomers *alone* understood the beauty of that.

In those grandiose septentrional forests that stretched, like an infinite cathedral of verdure, from Hudson Bay to the Gulf of Mexico; among the savage sublimity of the Rocky Mountains or over the beautiful slopes of the Andes to the banks of the Amazon or on the enchanted Antilles isles in the Caribbean Sea: in the middle of that unimaginable streaming of light, innumerable beings made in the resemblance of the Most High writhed in the blood-soaked mud of human sacrifices and agonized with terror under the implacable azure of that firmament that recounted no stories of divine glory to their poor souls!... O just God! five thousand years of that hell![21]

Theologians teach us that, in the other hell, punishment by privation of God infinitely surpasses all other punishments, and one of the greatest Fathers of the Church has come to tell us that man's soul is "naturally Christian." Those poor wretches then had, to the deepest degree of their moral blindness, some sort of presentiment of an absolutely *necessary* and absolutely inaccessible sovereign! Who then would dare to fix the exact limit that might separate the two abysses, as both one and the other could be called a "land of misery and tenebrous land, covered by the shadow of death; where no order is found and no redemption, but where sempiternal horror resides."?[22]

---

[21] Original footnote: 20,000 victims annually in Mexico alone, according to Clavigero.

[22] Original footnote: Matins for the dead – 3rd nocturn.

V

One day, finally, the Lord called on a man, as he had called on John to prepare the way,[23] and he invested in him, for a time, his power, in order that he might put an end, once and for all, to that semblance of dolorous eternity by which Satan, nicknamed the ape of God, had tried to ape him himself in a sacrilegious counterfeiting of his proper realm.

That man whom Isaiah seems to have in mind whenever he talks about distant islands and peoples at the extremities of the earth, it is Christopher Columbus, "the gentlest of men," like the Holy Spirit, as Moses said. The title Great Admiral, under which he was so calumniated in his lifetime, has no meaning anymore for a generation not familiar with his history. The masses know no more about him than his very mysterious name and... nothing else, except that he had doubled the size of the Earth and that men had assassinated him by the sorrow he felt in obscurity.

As for his providential and unique mission that ranks him among the half-dozen exceptionally prodigious men on whom divine Wisdom counted, who then would think about it, in this century inimical to greatness, if the Church, ever mindful and always great, did not think about it?...

The *Catholic* Church which is the Empress of the Orient and Occident and which carries in its name the universality of its right, has never forgotten any-

---

[23]John: John the Baptist, precursor of the Christ.

one; but it remembers more particularly, more deeply, and with more fervent delectation those among its children who have enlarged it and whom it enlarges in turn by honoring them under the twelve-times august vocable of Apostles.

"Has there ever been," said Christopher Columbus' historian, "a greater man than him who imitated nobody and whom nobody will be able to imitate for the duration of the globe?" Christopher Columbus' discovery of the New World, it was as if he had said to the Church: "Blessed Mother, I give to you, in the Name of Jesus Christ, half the earth. I give to you millions of souls whom I have given birth to for Salvation and who are the infinitely dolorous flowers of my spiritual entrails. I entrust them to you forever so that they might be brought back to the truth that they have fallen away from, like apostate angels, so many centuries ago. Those there are the divine Foundlings of Love whom I am the Messiah of and whom I symbolize in my name."

"Embrace those children and wrap your maternal arms around them," said the Lord, "until I come and until I show them mercy, because *my fountains overflow* and because my grace is inexhaustible."[24]

It was even as if he had said to the human spirit: "I double the extent of your inheritance and I enlarge the field, incredibly, already so vast, of your investigations. It is through me that 'a new meaning:

---

[24]Original footnote: 4 Ezra 2:32.

the meaning of great things and of the infinite'[25] will be suddenly revealed. Perfect consciousness of a terrestrial globe will be the least fruit of my discovery. I will give rise to the boldest scientific enterprises in the extraordinary centuries that follow. The book of nature, hermetically closed to date, has been finally opened and opened by me, the Discoverer of Creation, who will be, however, disdained and misjudged and who will disappear like a common torch carried into the wind of the tempest. I foresee that men will abuse that new gift of God just as they have abused all other gifts. But I also know that his will must be done for his kingdom will come in the end on this predestined earth that I have been made responsible to amplify and round out like an imperial sphere for Jesus Christ's future domination."

Christopher Columbus' greatness is so unique and inordinate that it disconcerts enthusiasm even, and it causes the ordinary framework of analogies, traditionally required for sainthood, even in the most exceptional ways, by theologians and ascetic doctors, – to break down. Later on I will discuss, in a rapid examination of the life of God's Servant, how that plenipotential Ambassador of the Holy Trinity, – misunderstood everywhere and loathed by Spain whom

---

[25]Original footnote: Humboldt, *Cosmos*, tome II, p. 321. – One will pardon me, I hope, in consideration of the pleasure of citing Humboldt, the small, but rather serious inconvenience of putting into the mouth of the Christian hero a word lacking in philosophical precision. It is without a doubt useless to point out that Columbus would have smiled at a CREATED *infinity*, the only, evidently, that the Prussian savant had in mind, and the only also that might really be conformant with the philosophical and political genius of his nation.

he had gorged with riches and power; exposed to miserable ecclesiastical persecutions, – will meet with sympathies and recomfort only at the pontifical Court and on the infallible Chair of Saint Peter. In the celebrated edition of *Ptolemy's Geography* published in Rome by Evangelista Tosino, in 1608,[26] the new continent named *"Terra* SANTCÆ CRUCIS,[27] as if that discovered world had been the sweetest fruit of the bleeding Tree of Redemption so as to be left to ripen on the branch for fifteen centuries longer than others. That fact is no less conclusive for a deep intelligence than for a mystical heart.

Christopher Columbus was a man of desire in the manner of Daniel. Now, desire calls out for desire, just as the abyss invokes the abyss "by the voice of God's cataracts" which are the torrents of tears of prayer and love: one year before the Discovery, he who was going to make the Church benefit the most from it was born: Saint Ignatius of Loyola; and, in the month when God's Ambassador was recalled by his master, seventeen days before his death, the apostle charged with executing his vow to evangelize the idolatrous nations appears in the world : Saint Francis

---

[26] *Ptolemy's Geography*... 1608: apparently published in Rome by Evangelista Tosinus, bookseller, possibly in 1508, rather than 1608, under this title (in Latin): *In hoc opere haec continentur Geographiae Cl. Ptolemaei: a plurimis uiris utriusq[ue] linguae doctiss. eme[n]data, & cu[m] archetypo Graeco ab ipsis collata.*

[27] *Terra sanctæ crucis*: Latin for "land of the holy cross."

Xavier.[28] [29] Those coincidences have nothing fortu-
itous about them. They are, on the contrary, infinitely
calculated and infinitely sage, that is to say, providential, like all things in this world. When a man is suscitated for the fulfillment of a portion of that grandiose
divine plan that is called History, it suffices for him to
reach out with both hands, like a blindman, to find his
instruments. But if that man is of Christopher Columbus' stature, he need not even make a move. It is a
gravitational focus for the multitude of souls who correspond with his destiny and who are mysteriously
orbited by him like a glorious constellation of spiritual satellites!

VI

I have just written that great word Desire which fills
the entire Old Testament like a prodigious sigh. I
could have compared Christopher Columbus' desire
to that of the Spirit that is shown to us in the Gospel
under the form of a dove[30] and which "postulates for
us," says Saint Paul, "with inexpressible plaintive
crying." What to say now or rather what to conjecture
of the desire of an entire world oppressed and stunned
stupid by the most satanic despotism, but at the heart
of which, nevertheless, the human soul, "inexter-

---

[28]Original footnote: *The Ambassador of God and Pope Pius IX*,
by the Count Roselly de Lorgues, p. 156. – [editor E.] Plon, 1874.

[29]seventeen days before his death. It may have been more than
seventeen if Xavier was born April 7, 1506, and Columbus died
May 20, 1506.

[30]dove: *colombe* in French.

minable" and naturally desirous, emits still, while vacillating, some glimmers?

It is written that the Lord "fulfills the desire of the poor," that never so lamentable a group of poor people had been seen before. However dark and deep their darknesses, it is not possible that a vague shiver of hope and desire had not risen up from the bottom of those miserable poor people's heart. After all, were they not the sons of Japheth and, by consequence, participants in the promise made to humankind? Although their separation from the rest of the Babelic congregation goes back to extremely ancient times, they had to have conserved amongst themselves something of an indeterminate thread of light, of infinite tenuity and pallor; and God, who knows the poor hearts he has created, well knows that that was enough for those abandoned people to continue desiring! But what were they desiring? They did not know at all. A sort of ancient tradition spoke only of extraordinary men who were supposed to come from the direction of the Orient and who would change everything in their country. Still, that deaf and mute expectation would give them more fear than joy. For them, that is what the Prophet Haggai's "*Veniet Desideratus*"[31] boiled down to.

The great English orator, Father Faber,[32] remarked how strange it was that there were *seven* days

---

[31] *Veniet Desideratus*: Haggai 2:8. Latin for "The Desired One will come."

[32] P. Faber: Frederick William Faber (AD 1814-63), an English theologian and writer who converted from Anglicanism to Roman Catholicism.

during which Our Lord did not have a name.[33] That *genesis* of the redoubtable Name, which made all submit, lasted more than two times seven centuries for the Americans and, admittedly, one can really say, without abusing the thrice-holy Word, that it is primarily for them that Jesus Christ was truly the "pontiff of *future* goods," divine appellation that Saint Paul, moreover, declares uninterpretable, on account, he says, of our imbecility.[34] The Christ, whom Tertullian[35] assures us every human soul bears within himself the presentiment and testimony of, was then, for those abandoned peoples, a perpetually anonymous God who could have overwhelmed them merely by the enigmatic and derisive *literality* of his promises!

It was the triumph and superb defiance of the Father of Lies, nowise anonymous, him, in his Gehenna, given that he bore all the horrible names inspired by the delirium of terror, and nowise enigmatic either given that he promised absolutely nothing to his deplorable slaves pressed by tortures and secularly discouraged from every precise and certain hope.

Given that Michael, vanquisher of the Devil, is designated in Scripture as "the great prince who stands up for the sons of God's people,"[36] is it not permitted to suppose him, hovering over those un-

---

[33]Original footnote: from Noel to the Circumcision.

[34]Original footnote: Hebrews 5:2; 9:11.

[35]Tertullian: Quintus Septimus Florens Tertullianus (AD 155-220), an early Christian theologian of Carthage.

[36]Original footnote: Daniel, 12:1.

known regions and preserving them from definitive despair, one of the companions of the Chief of Heaven, one of those angels of patience and sorrow, – like him who recomforted the Son of Man in the garden of agony, – whom artists depict for us in tears on the tombs of great people and whom a poor soul of a poet called, in his anguish, the "Dark Seraphim" of adversity? That spirit, vested with inexpressible divine pity for those peoples so heavily punished, and incorruptible confidant of the eternal design to deliver them in their turn, – without knowing when that time might be, – with what anguish-filled looks must he have looked at that desert of waves and that inaccessible horizon of azure, through which the Messenger of Salvation would come one day, like the Saint Christopher[37] of pious images, with Christ on his shoulders and the Holy Cross in hand!

And when the time had come, and, in the immaterial eyes of that tutor of so many desolate souls, the three small vessels of the lost Christ-Bearer appeared,[38] as if drowned in the immensity of the waves: the Hero who commanded them through so much suffering and with so steadfast a heart, – menaced by his muttering and frightened crews, torn perhaps by the fear of being unable to make himself obeyed, – he must have felt himself suddenly reimmersed in his steadfastness on hearing the celestial voice that spoke to his heart:

---

[37]Saint Christopher: a Christian martyr, purportedly dead in 251 AD, often depicted with Christ the child sitting on his shoulder.

[38]three small vessels...: the Niña, the Pinta, and the Santa Maria.

"Take courage, good Admiral, the men who surround you are nothing more than waves, moving and full of noise like those of the Ocean, and the Christ, your Lord, has decided that you would command the waves. Lift yourself up and dream on those *who are sleeping* under unknown isles. Remember your Message to the captive peoples who, so long in the shadows, wait for you. Consider what they suffer, and measure, if you can, to their ineffable distress, the greatness of God who chose you to act as a father to them by *standing in* for HIM HIMSELF! Their souls are so darkened and bent towards hell that they no longer know whether there is a heaven. The master who retains them behind his cursed gates, will he prevail then in the end against the shining Church of Jesus Christ? Those sad peoples are, at this very hour, like a multitude of wandering tombs in each of which repose the cadaver of deceased virtue while waiting for the great day when you come and resuscitate them. Messenger of the Almighty, are you yourself going to become, by heart failure, a silent sepulture? When Jesus, Father of the Poor, went to meet his celestial Clarifier, he promised that he would not abandon his orphan children and that he would come for them. Here it is now fifteen centuries since he departed, and the poorest among the poor wait for their father. Thousands of saints have wept for them, without knowing them. The Virgin Mother wept as well, and they are the sons of her greatest tears. The stars even of that beautiful sky that you contemplate for the first time, those brilliant and inanimate creatures have an appearance of sympathizing with so much ill fortune and shedding each night, on those exiles, their pale glimmers resembling tears of light. Take comfort, good servant. If you were going to perish! you, their only hope, what would become of them, and what would the Holy Mother Church do, for whom you are that unique and chosen Dove that is mentioned in the Canticles of Love?"[39]

And now that the internal Voice has made itself heard by that apostle and while it vibrates still in our hearts, despite the thickness of the centuries, let us ask ourselves what could be the true title and true name of the incomparable man whom the Church wants to honor, the liturgical vocable of our true glory. It seems to me that there is no other word than Father, and I shiver while writing that divine Name. Immediately after the Galilean fisher whom one calls the common Father of the faithful, what man of clay would ever have so many children and so prodigious a dilatation of paternal feeling.[40] Christopher Columbus was truly the father of the countless peoples he had gone out to find himself, like a very diligent Pastor, in the depths of that redoubtable Occident and barred by the monstrous swarming of the Abyss.

---

[39]Original footnote: *Una est* columba *mea, perfecta mea, una est matris suae, electa genetrici suae.* – Song of Songs 6:8.

[40]Original footnote: At the time of baptism of the seven Indians led by Columbus to Barcelona on return from his first voyage, the King, the infant Don Juan, and the first personages of the court were the godparents of the catechumens. As for Christopher Columbus, acting as the father of all Indians, he was the godfather of none of them; because in the Catholic Church a father cannot act as the godfather to his own son. (*History of Christopher Columbus*, by the Count Roselly de Lorgues. Book One, chapter XI.)

Saint Patrick, the apostle of green Ireland, heard, it is said, the cries of children in the belly of their mothers who called to him in Hibernia. During the terrible eighteen years of efforts that preceded his first voyage to India, Christopher Columbus carried in his soul the enormous clamor of half the human race whose existence he alone knew about and whom he wanted to give to Jesus Christ. To be more profoundly the father of those unfortunate people, he put on the poor habit of Saint Francis, and he wore it ostensibly until his death. Finally, when he had exhausted everything that the Father of fathers had left him of the thick lees at the bottom of his chalice of agony, when he had sufficiently seen the traffic and massacre of those whom he had drawn from his intestines, – his terrestrial destiny being suddenly accomplished, – that incomparable Resemblance of God sank down to die, making no more sound than an atom that crumbles from the height of a ruin in the desert...

Was not the immense pity and immense human misery of such a death needed so that that divine artist whom one calls the Church could have proposed to us, after four hundred years of distance, – like the arresting image of the Father of mercy – so majestic a physiognomy of a saint, so labored and devastated by suffering, so dripping with the spit of calumny, without fear or scandal for the fierce and stupid egoism of our Christian mores?

VII

The Dove of Noah, sent three times over the earth after the Deluge by the Holy Patriarch, "did not come back again" after the third time, says the Holy Book in its divine and mysterious language. That Dove, symbolic figure of the Spirit of the Lord who speaks to men through his prophets, flew down from the Ark towards the poor planet in mourning which the frightening *Repentance* of the Creator had submerged in the waters of his anger, as the penitent King one day had to moisten and *wash his bed* with the abundance of his tears. That visit to the earth by the Mystical Bird, is it not a palpable image of the written Word visiting men in the crepuscular half light of the law of expectation? In view of that unique masterwork that is called the Incarnation, eternal Wisdom was ineffably *reduced* to human language over the course of four thousand years. That language thus divinized was put into the mouth of the prophets, "like a sharpened sword and like a chosen arrow," so as to pierce all hearts and traverse all centuries. The dead language of men became, by a miracle of resurrection, the living Word of God and was restituted in that new form to the wandering and discouraged workers of ancient Babel. While those exiles made a confused noise over all the earth where they multiplied the babblement of their dementia, God alone spoke for the universality of peoples and times...

He came one day, he came one hour, waited for by seventy generations and providentially marked in the middle of the centuries, when that Word, assuming finally the liable flesh of the children of Adam, manifested itself to all nations and descended to *ask back again,* itself, its flock, just as Ezekiel had foretold. It is then that the Redeemer, impatient to die and needing to exercise, for so short a time, his ministry as supreme Pastor, chose his apostolic coadjutors to exercise it after him, once he had returned to his Father. And to confirm them in the faith, he placed above them one man, invested with the sublime Pontificate, exceptionally predestined, whose Name, full of mystery (*Barjona*), recalled that Dove of the Patriarch that was supposed to rest forever on his head and that of his successors.

The grandiose evangelical scene and the sacred words of the Master, by which the first of all Popes received possession of the keys and investiture of sovereign authority, are known throughout the universe. For nineteen centuries, the Mother Church teaches and chants alternately to its most ignorant children the sublime protestations of the Father's love, his Renunciation followed by such large tears, his immense apostolic works among Jews and Gentiles, his imprisonment and the miracle of his deliverance amidst so many other miracles, finally his magnificent symbolic crucifixion, Head downwards, as if to signify the taking root, into the earth, of the Doctrine of the Prince by priests of the new law, while his Feet pointing heavenwards make an expressive commentary on the *Sequere me*[41] of the Gospel.

Saint Peter had governed successively the Church of Jerusalem and that of Antioch where the faithful prayed for the first time as *Christians*, when, in the second year of the reign of Claudius, the seven hundred ninety-fifth year since the founding of Rome, and the forty-second of the common era, he came, by

---

[41] *Sequere me*: Latin for "Follow me."

the Lord's command, to settle in Rome. The immense empire of iron, foretold by Daniel, seemed to have broken and dominated everything on earth, in accordance with that Prophet's text. The time of that mysterious *stone* had come when, after having freed itself from the mountain, it would succeed in smashing to pieces the fragile feet of the colossus. That is why the Prince of Apostles went from Orient to Occident carrying in his hands the candelabrum of true belief and, in his veins of a future martyr, the empurpled seed of Catholicism. Paganism at that time was haughty and dense like the clouds of its Olympus, and the ancient Slave, despairing, like Pilate, of the truth, wallowed with fury in all the mud of superstition and impudicity. Hundreds of people sweated their agony and, in a supernatural discouragement, prostrated themselves at the granite or brass feet of Molochs or Cynocephaluses. It could not be that so great a multitude of human creatures were given over and abandoned to so terrible a disfiguration of the Image of God, without any help!...

At that moment, Simon-Peter, the Galilean of Bethesda and Capernaum, the fisher of fish having become the fisher of men, casts his net over the world and renews the miraculous catch, accomplishing thus for Jesus Christ the magnificent Unity of that Roman City that the Bronze Wolf had for eight hundred years given breast to, for the belly of Caesars. From Rome, he governs the nascent Church in Asia, in Greece, in Italy, in the Gauls, and as far as the coasts of Africa. He makes two trips to Jerusalem, shaking his flaming torch everywhere, standing up to the proud, giving strength to the poor and never stopping to shed the immortal tears of his penitence that flowed for thirty-four years. Finally, under Nero's reign, first persecutor of the Church, they arrest, like incendiaries of Rome, the disciples of Him who had declared that he wanted to "spread fire o'er all the earth"; the two greatest Apostles, Peter and Paul, prefigured previously by the two Columns of so pure a work that decorated the Holy Temple's portico,[42] – they are locked up together for nine months in the Mamertine Prison, at the foot of Capitoline Hill, and on June 29 in the year of grace 67 they receive, the both of them, the martyr's crown, the one by the sword, the other by the ignominious cross for slaves.

Such is the history of Peter, such the entire history of the Papacy. All popes are *Barjona*, that is to say, *sons of the Dove* which inspires them and through which they are veritably Vicars of Him who wanted to be recognized as the Son of God in virtue of that sign. All popes are that supreme and indefectible Pastor through whom others are confirmed and without whom they are not even phantoms of pastors. All are *fishers of men* and miraculous fishers. All weep for the famous Renunciation by which they have been warned of the fragility of the human tabernacle on the most elevated of thrones. All finally are crucified in a spiritual way corresponding with the crucifixion of Peter, who did not find that the Cross of the Master was so vile for his servant but who devised turning it upside down so that his successors, humiliated and suffering in him, could never be interrupted in their consideration of things from heaven's

---

[42]Original footnote: 3 Kings 7:21.

perspective!

VIII

Everyone in the world knows, especially in Italy, the already legendary fact of Pius IX's Dove. That fact, taken by a rather large number of enthusiastic souls for a sort of miracle, merits being retold because it expresses rather distinctly the persistent beauty and strength of one of the most ancient forms of Christian symbolism.

In the month of June 1846, Gregory XVI having just died, the cardinal Mastai Ferretti, then archbishop of Imola and Pope fifteen days later, arrived in Rome for the Conclave. "Traveling through Fossombrone, small village in the Marches, the carriage, stopped for several instants, was naturally surrounded by the crowd. A prince of the Church is always a spectacle, and principally at a moment of vacancy in the Holy See, where any cardinal can be elected Pope. Suddenly, descending out of the air from above, a white dove comes to rest on the carriage. The crowd claps their hands and bursts out with the expressive acclamation familiar to people of the pontifical states: 'Evviva! Evviva!' But as their cries did nowise frighten the dove, the spectators got it into their heads that that apparition was a presage. Some perhaps recall that future king of Rome, Tarquin the Elder,[43] on whom an eagle rested at the moment when, for the

---

[43]Tarquin the Elder: Lucius Tarquinius Priscus, 616-579 BC. An eagle was said to have descended on him, flown away with his cap, and then returned it to his head later.

first time, he arrived in the eternal city; others think of Pope Saint Fabien, whom a dove also had designated to the suffrages of the people and bishops, and the acclamations redouble: '*Evviva! Evviva*! Behold the Pope!' One person takes a long reed, as they grow along the ditches in Italy, and strikes the bird gently: it flies away, but it returns, retakes its place on the carriage, and rests immobile. Then the enthusiasm is at its greatest: 'Yes, behold the Pope! the Pope of the dove!' They followed them to the city gates. Only then did the bird take off in flight again and go to repose on the very gate of the prison, where several political prisoners were detained."[44]

However it might please critics to receive that *anecdote,* and even supposing it to be apocryphal, it is nonetheless confirmative of the universally accredited opinion that the popes are, in a manner, chosen and *hatched* by the baptismal bird that symbolizes evangelically the divine Third Person. As for Pius IX, two-hundred-sixtieth successor to Peter, – the only pope who exceeded the twenty-five years of Roman episcopacy of the Prince of Apostles, contrariwise to a tradition consecrated to a certain point by the liturgy itself in the ceremony of the coronation of popes, – his reign had been marked by such exceptional signs that it is impossible to be surprised by the exceptional predilection of that *son of the Dove* for Christopher Columbus.

The hierophant Fourier has given this abbreviated formula of human solidarity: "Attractions are

---

[44]Original footnote: Villefranche. – *Pius IX, His Life, His Story, His Century*, pp. 20-21.

proportional to destinies." It is one of the strongest expressions from that Æolian era so full of vain words, and it pleased God that those words should be proffered by a mouth that could be called the most enormous *vomitorium* of human error of the nineteenth century.

The destiny of Columbus and the destiny of Pius IX meet and interpenetrate in the mystery of a supernatural exception. Columbus reveals the sphericity of the terrestrial world beneath the feet of Jesus Christ and his Mother; Pius IX, by the cathedral definition of two great dogmas that the transcendental harmony of theological teaching still lacked,[45] has closed that glorious circle of light that envelops human intelligences in exile, – like the splendid ring of that planet of silence and melancholy that rolls so prodigiously distant from us in the depths of the sky!

"And other sheep I have, that are not of this fold," said the good Pastor, and "them also I must bring, and they shall hear my voice; and there shall be one fold, and one shepherd."[46] It is evident that those two immense, predestined men, Christopher Columbus and Pius IX, were suscitated, at three hundred years of distance, in view of preparing and rendering, immediately following, that holy and marvelous Unity that Holy Scripture calls the "desire of everlasting hills."[47] The first destroyed forever the barrier that divided the flock, and the second, with his luminous

---

[45]two great dogmas...: Pope IX revived the dogma, dating from the Middle Ages, of the Virgin Mary's Immaculate Conception; as well he promulgated the dogma of Papal Infallibility.

[46]And other sheep.... one shepherd: John 10:16.

and paternal hand that poured the blood of the Son of God over nations, designated infallibly for all future centuries the true place and true name of that unique Pastor.

The intervention of the idea of Providence, in examination of historical facts, has, for ordinary effect on the human spirit, the immediate abolition of the notion of time. In the plan of eternal designs, all men are contemporaries. Pius IX and Christopher Columbus correspond sympathetically the one to the other following a spiritual law identical with the physical law of the attraction of worlds. It has been remarked that Pius IX, who believed in the saintliness of Columbus and who was the promoter of that unprecedented cause, is the only one of all the popes who has visited the American continent. When Abbot Mastai, still a simple priest, accompanied the nuncio sent by Pope Pius VIII to Chili in order to re-establish ecclesiastical affairs in that distant country, the future pope ought to have felt growing in him that marvelous appetite for divine glory by which the boldest child of the Church had formerly rolled out the entire earth like a rug of kingdoms before the feet of the Redeemer. For two years, he visited the missions of Chili, Peru, and Columbia, at the cost of great fatigues and even greater dangers, realizing in that way a new sort of apprenticeship of that ever-growing Papacy that the Discoverer of the New World had rendered similar to a Rhodian Colossus of Paternity standing on two hemispheres.

The Count Roselly de Lorgues asks, "who is

---

[47]the desire... hills: Genesis 49:26.

the canonized saint that, before Christopher Columbus, anticipated the dogma of the Immaculate Conception and ordered the construction of a church in its
honor." It would evidently be quite pointless to try to
make men grudgingly understand the infinite importance of that Definition, which would suffice in and
of itself for the glory of the Church and all its popes,
by supposing that the wisdom of all its councils and
the inspiration of all its learned doctors had never
been capable of producing anything but that unique
suffrage of truth and love!

As for the other dogma that had so stirred contemporary pride and made so much original mud rise
to the surface of hearts, it would be a sort of derision
to write that the Servant of God had simply anticipated it, he who never counted on anything but Rome to
be understood and to be confirmed. In the famous affair of the Line of Demarcation where the peace of
Christianity and the future of the world were in question, and which was the occasion of one of the greatest miracles in history, Christopher Columbus wanted
no other arbiter than the Holy See, at the time occupied by that same Pope whose name alone has the
privilege of making foam at the mouth and chomp at
the indignant bit the virtuous flock of apocalyptic on-
agers of free thought and the history of free thought.
Rome, in turn, through the mouth of the Pontiff,
whose memory is nowise abhorrent to the Holy
Church, adopted spontaneously the Navigator's con-
clusions and lent to him full credence in extraordinary, unverifiable things, which were of immense
consequence; giving back, in this way, to that Messenger of Christ, by an exception without example,

the almost divine honor of an arbitrage that was his absolute privilege and his sacred prerogative.[48]

Certainly, there has never been any saint in whose eyes Rome was more indubitably the CHURCH. Christopher Columbus thought only of her and worked only for her unto his dying day. His miraculous story is no other than the Odyssey of that magnificent solicitude that makes him resemble Saint Paul so much. Barely disembarked from his first voyage of discoveries, his first step was to counsel Catholic Kings to pay homage to the Holy See for its new lands and to entice its benediction over that enterprise with a bull that would protect its conquests. And it was like that for the entire remainder of his life, his admirable heart tending towards Rome and having never been able to consider Spain, which had become great because of him, as anything other than the most precarious of ungrateful countries and perhaps even as the stopgap of God's mercy!

IX

For all these reasons and for a rather large number of others that are easily deducible from history, it is clear that the Pope of the Dove should naturally be attracted to that *Dove*.[49] Without being a millenarian exactly, it is permitted to believe in the future triumph of that Spirit of love that the dove is the symbol of,

---

[48]Original footnote: See Appendix A.

[49]Dove: In French, *colombe* means "dove," and *Colomb* refers to Christopher Columbus.

which the Church constantly evokes and which must teach us every truth, by the testimony of Our Lord in the Gospel of St. John. Christopher Columbus and Pius IX seem to belong more specially than others to that imminent accomplishment of the kingdom of God among men. Also, the enthronement of that great pope had been the point of departure for the movement of Catholic opinion in favor of Columbus. The spirit that blows where it will has passed over that irremediably broken reed, over that torch that no longer smolders even, and, all of a sudden, the name become almost banal of Christopher Columbus has taken on a new meaning and has begun to resplend like a meteor.

What follows is the very rapid summary of the progress of that rehabilitation.

Since the year 1846, date of Pius IX's elevation to St. Peter's Chair, an incredible number of publications and works of art of all sorts, relative to Columbus,[50] attested in diverse parts of the Christian world to an immediate and singular preoccupation of universal consciousness, when in 1856, the first complete history of the Christian hero, edited by order of the Sovereign Pontiff, was published in Paris and laid out the hagiographic question in a definitive manner, without any bias however and under absolute reserve of the infallible decision of religious authority.

I said it at the beginning: that book caused in our little-believing society all the noise that one could expect from so firmly a Catholic publication. The renown of that renascent Christian glory spread

---

[50]Original footnote: See Appendix B.

throughout the world whose greatness was divulged by that poor *Genoese pilot*. One was surprised by the supernatural nimbus that came to illuminate suddenly that sorrowful and grandiose figure, emerging from an obscurity of four centuries by the voice of the Pastor of souls. Faithful hearts that know what a saint is and how important to God it is to be glorified among his elect, exulted on hearing that news and wanted finally to know the true life and the true mission of that Discoverer of America in the only Catholic recitation that had been written. Nonetheless, Count Roselly de Lorgues' work, now more than a quarter of a century old, is still too little known.

The only one, perhaps, of all Catholic writers who might hold some credit among the Philistines of Free Thought, the brilliant novelist-critic Jules Barbey d'Aurevilly spoke about it on the day following its appearance and, by a rare prophetic intuition, saw it for what it was, large in all its consequences, and announced it for what it has really become, that is to say: "the official statement of a future canonization." That isolated testimony had, to be honest, little effect on the tenebrous cesspool of contemporary indifference. Here and there, journals hostile to the Redemption proffered insults and inept raillery. The *History of Christopher Columbus* ran, as it could, its fortune. Until 1869, epoch of the Postulation, the episcopacy was almost alone in being moved by it almost everywhere. Today, that book has passed through a larger number of hands. The recent publication by the *Li-*

brairie Catholique[51] will, doubtless, accelerate that tardy popularity, and it will be quite necessary that the people of the world let themselves be gripped by it in turn, for the truth, divine substance of love, is strong and conquering like death.

In an extremely remarkable letter that occupied the European press for some time in 1866, Monseigneur the Cardinal de Bordeaux, metropolitan of the bishops of the Antilles, supplicated the Sovereign Pontiff to authorize the introduction of the Cause for Christopher Columbus before the Sacred Congregation of Rites. The greater part of the French Episcopate supported by its vows the procedure given by the venerable cardinal whom France now mourns. A certain number of bishops gave their formal support to the letter by His Eminence. Ecclesiastics of various dioceses added their voices to those of the first pastors. The Spanish press itself supported that project of Beatification, in a strange contradiction of the disdain and secular hatred of that nation for its benefactor. His Eminence the Cardinal-Archbishop of Bruges extended to his colleague de Bordeaux *patriotic* congratulations in the name of the Spanish Episcopate, and joined his personal backing to the request for Beatification. In America, that idea was accepted with favor by the press of various states. In Brazil, it inspired a poet. In the two continents, many Protestant countries showed their frank warmth for the Cause for

---

[51]Original footnote: A magnificent in-quarto vol. with frames on each page and chromo-lithographies; published by Victor Palmé of the *Société générale de librairie catholique*. All the same, that luxurious book has the disadvantage of being merely an abridgment of the edition published by Didier.

Christopher Columbus. In Russia even, at the seat of orthodox deceit, the idea of such a Beatification produced a sensation echoed in its accredited rags.

Many bishops having then meditated on the life of Christopher Columbus wrote directly to His Holiness. From the sea of the Antilles and from the Indian Ocean, appeals were addressed to Rome. On the example of the illustrious Archbishop of Mexico, many heads of diocese, in America as in Asia, without having drafted their appeal, backed wholeheartedly that most eminent Cardinal Donnet. The superior generals of religious orders seconded those pious hopes by their vows. In the following year, one of the most learned and most renowned prelates of Italy, Monseigneur Andrea Charvaz, archbishop of Genoa, addressed in turn, to the Sovereign Pontiff, a letter in which, recognizing the extreme difficulties that introduction of the Cause for Christopher Columbus presents, by consequence of the necessity to conform to rules put in place by Pope Benedict XIV, he supplicated His Holiness to use his sovereign authority in order to introduce that most exceptional cause by exceptional means.

Finally, convocation of the œcumenical Council at Rome seemed to offer to representatives of the Church a favorable occasion to award a mark of gratitude to that heroic Christian. M. the Count Roselly de Lorgues, official postulator, although laic, addressed to the Fathers of the Council a Memorandum recalling the rights of Christopher Columbus in a solemn testimony of recognition. On the advice of a large number of archbishops, bishops, and councilors, a

Postulation was drawn up that supplicated the Head of the Church to defer to the wishes of the faithful and, using his apostolic sovereignty, to order the introduction of that Cause by exceptional means.

A certain number of prelates having left Rome immediately after their vote on Infallibility, it was agreed that as soon as the session resumed the Postulation would be proposed publicly for signing by the Fathers of the Council. Many among them had to make a motion relative to the Cause for Christopher Columbus. In a special work,[52] M. the Count Roselly de Lorgues has given the entire text of that Postulation which already bore the signature of cardinals, primates, archbishops, bishops, and apostolic vicars from different regions of the Globe; when the chastisement by France and the brutish intrusion of despoilers of the Holy See, by creating obstacles to the reunion of the œcumenical Assembly, adjourned that matter whose opportunity was so widely proclaimed.

The well-known veneration of Pius IX for that admirable servant of God, his pious desire to place his miraculous dust on the holy altars, and the unanimous and almost spontaneous acclamation by Fathers of the Council have then finally brought back Christians' attention, after ten years, to the story of Christopher Columbus. Today, that great Cause is more than ever pending before the Church. The Postulation has already received innumerable suffrages. From all points of the globe, more than SIX HUNDRED BISHOPS

---

[52]Original footnote: *The Ambassador of God and Pius IX*. – Plon, 1874. – the *Postulatum* reproduced at the end of the present work, Appendix C, may be recommended to minds most jealously amorous of the living Roman Latinity.

have sent their particular support to the Postulator.
Truly extraordinary number, and more than sufficient
to carry the universal support of Christianity.

That is, in a nutshell, the story of the Cause
for Christopher Columbus, Apostle of the Cross and
Messenger of Jesus Christ. God has not permitted
Pius IX to see the triumph of this on earth, but the
glory of having been the promoter of it remains his,
and the world will know one day just what a glory it
is. While we wait, the universal Church will pro-
nounce with all the strength of infallible authority that
it possesses from its Head, and the Holy Spirit that inspires him and that was formerly *borne* by Christopher Columbus *on the unexplored waters* of the
Ocean will know how to vanquish the latest obstacles
of ignorance or satanism, at the exact day and hour
marked by all eternity for that justice.

X

Some years ago, a bishop who humbly leaves his
piety to hover like an eagle above his intelligence re-
proached Christopher Columbus for not resembling
Saint Benedict Labre or the Curé d'Ars. Evidently,
that prelate is not like those men whom the silence of
the stars frightens, to quote Pascal.

Apart from that, he is a superior ecclesiastic among
the most correct and who must realize in a perfect
manner the Gallican ideal of devotion: *in pietate in-
signi minime singularis*. That is to say, the hatred of
all singularity, of all exception, of all transcendence;

the instinctive defiance of all enthusiasm and all mag-
nanimous strong emotion. For such spirits, the exalta-
tion of love is always an extravagant ridiculousness,
the lyricism of thought is a regrettable deliriousness,
and the most sublime apperceptions of genius are an
absurd studied elegance *from noon to two o'clock*. It
is in this way that they are pleased to express themselves.

As for their admiration for Saint Benedict
Labre and the Curé d'Ars, one must not put too much
stock in it. Saints have always been *singular* men,
said Massillon, and, to be sure, it appeared difficult to
be any more so than the famous mendicant pilgrim,
grown acceptable today because the Church has spoken and because it is more than one hundred years after his death, but who spent his life, as did the Curé
d'Ars, receiving lessons and reprimands from a
throng of wise and moderate men whose piety was
distinguished, without the least alloy or admixture of
singularity.

Every time God wants to make a very great
saint, he does it as he did with Job. He begins by
sending him small and facile tests, such as robbers,
fire, tempest, ruin, mourning, abandonment, nudity,
insult, dungheap, and the most horrible ulcers. Thus
far, nothing exceeds the common measure of human
strength, and the Devil alone has been unleashed. But
if those preliminary tests are endured with constancy,
if the subject has not sinned at all *by his lips*, then
God administers the supreme and definitive blow,
striking the man like a gold coin with his effigy on it
and which resembles loving caresses compared to all

that has gone on before. He simply makes some pious men, who are exempt from singularity and prodigious in wise counsels, intervene.

Christopher Columbus, more astonishing than Saint Laurent, endured that gridiron for eighteen years before his first expedition, and, from the time of the Discovery to that of his death, he knew no other softening than that of having been turned away by implacably virtuous hands.[53]

We are advised by the Lord himself to respect our bishops who are the successors of the Apostles, but, at the same time, the good Book makes it a precept for us to correct our friends and our neighbors: *Corripe amicum, corripe proximum.*[54] Who then is more a friend and neighbor to us than those who are charged with watching over us and instructing us, and how could the last sheep in the flock be justifiably

---

[53]Original footnote: I cannot resist the pleasure of reproducing here a curious page by one of the most singular and eloquent writers of that century. That page has this title: THE LETTER THAT A DOCTOR, A VERY SERIOUS MAN, HAD TO WRITE TO CHRISTOPHER COLUMBUS AT THE MOMENT HE EMBARKED FOR AMERICA. – "I learn, my young friend, that you have the plan of discovering a new world, and I will tell you without mincing words that I do not wish you the best. Your plan alarms me. It denotes, I am not afraid to say, an inconceivable pride. How dare you! Do you not find the world to be already large enough? See the men of past centuries. Have they ever dreamt of discovering a new continent? And you, you young man, without experience, without authority, you nourish within your breast that crazy ambition. (That young man without experience was already 57 years old.) How dare you! neither the counsels of all your true friends, nor the menaces of destiny that work against you, nothing can convince you to live tranquilly in Europe, like the rest of us. You believe yourself to be superior to other men given what suffices for them does not suffice for you? All enlightened people will tell you, my young friend, your pride will ruin you.

blamed when they throw themselves at assisting their pastor on the verge of failing? The discipline of the Church could not be offended by such a respectable audacity of language, and the history of holy bishops teems with examples of that charitable audacity that their humility knew how to profit from and which was for them the occasion of a redoubling of solicitude.

In the third part of this work, which will treat of several obstacles raised at the introduction of the Cause for Christopher Columbus, I would have too

---

"I am all the more chagrined by your deplorable obstinacy given I have always held a true affection for you. As a child, you pleased me. I loved the keenness and the promptitude of your witticisms. As a young man, you had an imagination that captivated me. For I love imagination in a young man provided it is not too much. You said to me sometimes: 'I love the Ocean!' and I encouraged you, my child, to write some Latin verses on the Ocean, by way of practice. Could I have imagined that you were going to take poetry seriously? If you had, moreover, so pronounced a taste for navigation, I would not have dissuaded you from taking from time to time several small voyages; voyages form youth. But, my young friend, permit me to ask you this: isn't it going a bit far to go searching for a new world?

"And why not be content with the old, given that we, we know how to content ourselves? Why not enter quite simply into one of those liberal careers that your education gives you the right to pretend to? Why this insane and ridiculous ambition? Ah! when you are my age!

"To which you have already responded that over there there are men who are your brothers whom you want to unite with the old continent.

"I know by heart all your grand phrases. You think, tell me it isn't so, that after you have traversed the Ocean that tries to separate two worlds, you will plant your Cross on new land.

many occasions of that sort of remonstrance not to warn from this moment in time timid spirits whom a similar *temerity* might scandalize or cause to suffer. They can dispense with reading me because it is not to them that I address myself. At the risk of covering myself in ridicule, I declare my ambition to speak only to souls unbounded by desire and enthusiastic

"Those there, my child, are empty words; permit a man older than you to make you see it. You know that I love the arts, and that I respect religion, but I don't love saints and men of genius: the one and the other go too far, they continually exaggerate. Europe has produced enough of them and even too many; they are good only for stirring up the world. What madness it is to go over there, at the risk of breaking your neck, to swell the ranks of dreamers! Be careful, my child, you are going to become ridiculous. Believe in the sincere affection that dictates these words to me, that I address to you. I cannot conceal to you the regret I feel when I see you lost, in the empty dreams of an insensate pride, a young man for whom I was pleased to dream of a better future.

"Yes, my child, my heart is aggrieved, when I see you going from door to door begging for the assistance that is refused to you. What have you done with your dignity? Your family's honor has been spotless until now. Do you lack all self-esteem now?

"Self-esteem, my child, is the guardian of dignity, and for a well-born man, dignity is the most precious thing he possesses. Without a doubt (because I don't want to exaggerate in anything), one must not have too much self-esteem, excess in everything is a fault, but one must have a little, and, if you continue, you will convince me that you no longer have any; take up, among us, one or another of those honorable public offices that your young intelligence will make you capable of succeeding at: in doing so, you will stop aggrieving your friends. Around you we will all be in agreement: we will encourage you in your enterprises, and we will slay the fat calf, on seeing the prodigal son return." ERNEST HELLO. – *Pans of the Balance* – p. 373.

[54]Ecclesiasticus 19:13-15.

like flames of love. It is the means for obtaining merely the twelve hundred readers dreamt of by the skeptic Stendhal, and, with the grace of God, that small number will have to suffice, if it enters into eternal designs that the Discoverer of Creation should finally be glorified on this ungrateful earth whose extent he doubled.

However, I cannot complete this section without speaking about another prelate whose excessive prudence would be unable to become an obstacle for the Cause, but who could with reason accuse me of an inexactitude if I had the appearance, by neglecting to note down his refusal, of counting him in the enormous number of episcopal adherents already mentioned.

Having sent the *Postulatum* to the archbishop of Auch, Monseigneur de Langalerie, the Count Roselly de Lorgues received, in the month of November 1879, a response from His Greatness that declared that he was unable to decide whether to sign that piece, he said, because of his insurmountable REPUGNANCE!... One month later, the same archbishop wrote that a *first serious success* obtained in Rome could *maybe* seal his adhesion.

Thus, the so well known and so formally expressed desire of Pius IX, the nearly unanimous acclamation of the Fathers of the Council, and the suffrage of the greater part of bishops around the world, finally the surprising concert of a multitude of sacerdotal or lay voices imploring that great act of justice from all points on the globe, – all that did not appear to Monseigneur d'Auch to be a suitably resounding bell, and he trembles to compromise himself while letting himself be preceded by nothing short of half the universe. The Cardinal-Archbishop of Bordeaux, the venerable and lamented pontiff who dared, the first, in the midst of universal silence, to supplicate Saint Peter's on behalf of Christopher Columbus, must have seemed strangely temerarious to him. Following the ideas of Monseigneur d'Auch, scruple in these sorts of affairs can never be carried too far, and, in supposing it excessive even, it is only just if it began to cease being insufficient. The Apostles, whom he has the honor of being one of the successors of, could well have the simplicity of doves, but it would be hazarding a great deal perhaps to attribute to them the prudence of serpents as recommended by the Master;[55] for, at the end of the day, they did not show that saintly episcopal *repugnance* which would have contained the juvenile fervor of their zeal, and we would not be reduced to asking ourselves today whether they would have done better to wait for a *first success* of Christianity to begin their predication.

Repugnance for the Cause for Christopher Columbus! Of course, I must remind myself that I am speaking at this moment of a venerable and virtuous pastor, of one of those men replete with honor whom the Pope calls my brother; but I cannot forget that the same astonishing word was pronounced, three years ago, at the parliamentary tribunal, I do not remember anymore by whose ignoble mouth, and it had to do with the Sacred Heart! Devotion to the Heart of Jesus

---

[55]Matthew 10:16: "Behold, I send you forth as sheep in the midst of wolves: be ye therefore wise as serpents, and harmless as doves."

Christ inspired repugnance in that champion! Well do I know that the rapprochement is appalling, but it is justified by the identity of the word, and the words have an inexorably substantial and revelatory metaphysic...

If Christopher Columbus is really a saint, – something that the Church does not prevent us from supposing, – it is quite frightening to have a like repugnance and more frightening still to be unable to surmount it. There, that is what I had to say respectfully to Monseigneur d'Auch whose character and eminent dignity I would be horrified to appear to disdain. I know quite well that that pious archbishop will adhere with all his heart to the Postulation once it has triumphed and that he will honor without repugnance Christopher Columbus when the Church inscribes his incomparable name in the sacred Diptychs; but then, doubtless, he will understand how much more honorable it would have been for His Greatness to have had a premonition of it and hastened that decision!

XI

I have already mentioned, a large number of times, the Postulator of the Cause, the Count Roselly de Lorgues. I must still name him and cite him often, given he is the principal worker of that great contemporary thing that will be regarded as one of the most beautiful *gestures* of God by France in the XIXth century. If the transcendent interest in the glory of Christopher Columbus did not immediately abolish around him every other historic or literary interest, that would be a second act of justice to recount the life and works of that Christian apologist, so famous in what I would call the *recto* of this century and now surpassed by the despicable crowd of oracular street performers of Anti-Christianity. But so vast an examination cannot be contained in a simple biographical parenthesis. More space is needed and less incidence to speak of a man who has philosophically *informed* half his contemporaries and who was the intellectual progenitor of Donoso Cortés.[56] It would suffice doubtless for the glory of the Count Roselly de Lorgues to have written the life of Christopher Columbus, as nobody perhaps would have written it in his absence until the day of Judgment; but, before being a historian, one ought to remember that he was the renovator of the ancient Christian apology that had been akin to the literary vagitus of the Church in the first three centuries. Only, he renewed that venerable genre by rejuvenating it and re-immersing it, like old Æson in the Fable,[57] in the enormous boiling vat of all scientific progress and human spirit. Monstrous and Babelian receptacle, image of profound Chaos before the Almighty's Verb had turned him into a henchman of the Light, everything was contained there and blended together in that mysterious, harmonic disorder that preceded ordinarily the great sudden order that Providence wants to operate!

---

[56]Cortés: Juan Cortés: AD 1809-1853, a Spanish Catholic conservative political philosopher and statesman.

[57]Æson in the Fable: Æson, of Greek myth, the father of Jason, of the Golden Fleece fable. Jason whose wife Medea slit Æson's throat and boiled the body in order to make him come back to life younger.

The Count Roselly de Lorgues profoundly discerned the vocation and religious mission of modern times, and he declared to the Athenians of his generation that having seen in passing the divers *simulacra* of their scientific cult, he had found, – like Saint Paul – *an altar dedicated to* THE UNKNOWN GOD, and that that object of their ignorant adoration was, assuredly, the Father of light and the God of sciences. And he demonstrated what he was affirming, glorifying science, for science would never have dared dream to glorify itself, placing it as a footstool under the Lord's feet, above the most inaccessible peaks of human pride, making it give breast, amorously, to the Catholic Tradition that the same pride pretended to extenuate through it; turning, finally, the famous temptation contained in the Gospel against that *denatured* daughter of the Father of Lies and promising her all empires in the world and all their glory if she consented to prostrate herself before the Son of God!

Less great a writer than Chateaubriand, unless by flashes of genius, less sharp and transpiercing than de Maistre, the Count Roselly de Lorgues has shown himself to be infinitely superior in doctrine compared to the first of these two eagles, and he grasps, he wraps his head around, better than the second, the truth he lays hold of or the error he wants to stifle.

The best known of his philosophical works, *Christ Before the Century*, has been translated into all languages. The two others, of posterior date, *Death*

Before Man,[58] and *The Cross in Two Worlds*, have had, in France, less resounding success, the first above all, I do not know why. *The Cross in Two Worlds* has this in particular that it was the point of departure for the great evolution by which its author became Christopher Columbus' historian. His providential role as Ambassador of God appeared to him simultaneously, and the surge of intuition that made him apperceive it was so completely illuminative that the strict and laborious study that came afterwards added practically nothing to that impulsive apperception.

The effect, moreover, was so contagious that it is to the *The Cross in Two Worlds* that the city of Genoa – shamefully ungrateful for the most illustrious of its sons, as I will demonstrate later – owes its monument to Christopher Columbus; monument erected by order of the King Charles-Albert, surprised by Genoese insouciance, after having read that book.

It was also the reason for the choice by Pius IX, who did not want any other historian for his predilect hero, whom the French writer favored by such historic sagacity and who justified thereby the incertitude of Joseph de Maistre, asking himself if the infallibility of Popes does not go beyond what one supposes and if it does not involve sometimes certain points extremely distant from the conjectures of Christian reason.

---

[58]Original footnote: Of all Count Roselly de Lorgues' apologetic books, *Death Before Man* is certainly that which justifies the most enthusiasm among his admirers and which explains best his influence on certain elevated minds of his time.

Today the Count Roselly de Lorgues, having reached the latter part of his life, could, so far as it seems, repose in the strength and in the serenity of his old age. He could regard his work as accomplished. He could say that his soul is fatigued by the weight of so long a day and leave to others the noble concern for triumph of truth on earth. But he considers in his capacity as a knight the extraordinary honor that he received, and he esteems, as is appropriate, the grandeur of his mandate. He feels that *all* his effort is needed and that he owes his last breath to that inexpressibly holy Cause, inasmuch as the human river needed to flow for four hundred years to the point that that clamor might rise up and reach God, that unique clamor of justice that the Lord God will not hear perhaps ever again!

So long as Christopher Columbus has not been *officially* restituted by the Church, the friend and faithful commissary that Pius IX is cannot rest, similar on this point to the great Apostle-Admiral who never thought that his work had been fulfilled and who rested only after death.

XII

The coming appearance of a new book by the Count Roselly de Lorgues – *Posthumous History of Christopher Columbus*, – which it appears to me ought to shed a blanket of light on a large number of unknown facts and superabundantly explicative of the surprising historic disgrace of the Christ-Bearer,[59] will give doubtless little joy to the hereditary enemies of that unequaled man, invested with the most solemn of all titles of eminent dignities, such as Viceroy of India and Great Admiral of the Ocean; titles necessary for the execution of sublime designs but which the revolting duplicity of an evil prince rendered illusory by never allowing him to exercise his authority and, soon thereafter, by depriving him of it completely with the atrocious cynicism of Renaissance politics. That truly exceptional book will be nothing other than the recitation of the improbable adventure of that exorbitant glory crashing and burning near its dawn, voyaging into the mystery of the catacombs beneath the rumbling of ten generations and shooting up suddenly by a Pope's will and in spite of the diabolical efforts of a multitude of imbeciles terrified by such a sign, at the precise and providential moment when the darkened splendor of Catholicism has so much need of that consolation of magnificence!

The indefatigable Postulator after having recounted, in the *History* of Columbus, the Christian Odyssey of him whom he calls the Messenger of the Gospel, will show us now the horrible, dark underside of that immense drama where weeping Angels were able to contemplate the abominable victory of powerful people crushing down a Poor man who was the friend of God. One will be able to see unfold, from that moment forward, thread by thread, the learned weft of that tissue of iniquities that starts with the first success of the Christian hero and that tends no less

---

[59]Christ-Bearer: from French "Porte-Christ" which, explained previously, is just the literal meaning of the name Christopher.

than to the total ruin, without remedy, of the most grandiose conceptions that the love of a man has ever conceived.

The indignant and implacable historian is not content with that whirlwind of crimes and lies which submerge, like waves, God's Envoy; he makes us stride over his coffin and forces us to grope in the dark over the forgotten sepultures of his race fallen completely into the same gulf. Of course! it suits God that truth and justice should finally have their turn, and that hypocrisy, even secular hypocrisy, should once and for all be unmasked, so that this earth that he made absolutely does not resemble any sinister Pantheon, on the door of which a hand from the Abyss might have written these words in the blood of the saints: HERE ONE ASSASSINATES GREAT MEN![60]

The earth has never loved those who dominate it, those who volplane above it, whether they be eagles or doves. "It furnishes the birdshot for killing them," said M. Hello somewhere. However, if one knows how to delve deeply into things, one would see that no one is closer to us and more like us than great men because they are the eldest sons of Him who fashioned us in his image and that they stand in front of him to shield us from the resplendent sun of his Face. The Apostle St. James, try as he may to tell us that Elijah was like us and liable,[61] we refuse to be-

---

[60]Here One Assassinates Great Men: this is also the title of a short monograph on Catholic author Ernest Hello that Léon Bloy wrote and published in 1895.

[61]The Apostle... Elijah: James: 5:17: Elijah "was a man subject to like passions as we are..." (KJV).

lieve it; not from humility, but because of the ignoble stupidity of our pride, which does not want to admire anything. The prejudice against Christopher Columbus is so tenacious and so strong that the greatest poet in the world, supposing him inspired by the most magnificent of all indignations, would never succeed in overcoming it. The Church alone has that power, because "its conversation is in heaven" and because, being the spouse of Jesus Christ and full of miracles, it knows the secret for loosening the heart of men of goodwill as well as the tongue of imbeciles.

God protects us from prejudging the infallible decision of that Mother of the living. She has remained silent to this day and, by consequence, we barely have the right to speak. But the trembling expression of a religious desire is not inimical to a profound respect and a filial submission. The Count Roselly de Lorgues, who has the honor of representing Christianity in his quality of Postulator of the Cause of Christopher Columbus, appeared destined for the even greater honor of seeing it triumph. He is permitted to consider as probable that the next session of the œcumenical Assembly will take up again, to bring it to completion, that great affair that, in turn, is there, now, like the Navigator's other great affair, "arms open, calling and waiting."[62] But the Postulator must be assisted by all Catholics, and he is saddened to think that, until present, he has seen himself stand-

---

[62]Original footnote: The question of Holy Places, one of the Admiral's most ardent preoccupations. – "El otro negocio famosisimo está con los 'brazos abiertos llamando: extrangero ha sido fasta hora.'" – Letter to Catholic Kings, dated from Jamaica, July 7, 1503.

ing almost alone. Ecclesiastical sympathies, beginning with the most august, have certainly not been lacking; but the world, the vast laic world has not been much moved thus far...

In recent years, the Count Roselly de Lorgues, fearing that he would not live long enough to sing the *Nunc dimittis* of victory and not wishing that that great thought should die with him, decided to choose a Vice-Postulator to continue his work after he passed. The selection was difficult and of grave consequence. A man of very sure mind and patient fervor was needed, whom neither the contradictions of the world nor the interminable delays of the Court of Rome would be able to put off. He cast his eyes and fixed his choice on a compatriot of the great man, M. Joseph Baldi, the *first* Genoese man to have written as a *Catholic* on Christopher Columbus. Issue of an ancient family transplanted to Genoa at the beginning of the XVIIth century, called on by his opulent commerce in precious stones to travel the seas, having passed many times from the Atlantic into the great Ocean, he could, with the Psalmist, admire the transports[63] of the sea, *mirabiles elationes maris*. During one of his voyages, as he was returning to Europe, having gotten past the terrible Cape Horn, his ship was assailed by the most frightening tempest. While everyone on board thought they were done for, that predestined Christian did not implore the assistance of Columbus' God in vain.

His long maritime pilgrimages had marvelously prepared M. Joseph Baldi to appreciate the gran-

---

[63]transports: emotionally speaking.

deur of him who, the first, dared to step out of the in-exorable Circle of Popillius[64] of traditional cosmography. When he read his history written by order of Pius IX, his soul was completely elated by the moral beauty of the Gospel's Messenger, and his enthusiasm made him a writer. M. Joseph Baldi is, of all Italians, the person who has worked the most efficaciously to spread throughout the Peninsula the Catholic glory of that Great Admiral of the Ocean. He merited by con-sequence the immense privilege that he shared, from then on, with one of the most significant defenders of the faith in the XIXth century.

In 1881, on Palm Sunday, M. Joseph Baldi was presented to His Holiness Leo XIII by the Count Roselly de Lorgues, and he had the honor of placing under the Pope's eyes a magnificent album, assuredly the most curious collection that had ever been brought into the Vatican. That album contained at that time FOUR HUNDRED SIXTY-SIX episcopal names in support of soliciting from the Head of the Church in-troduction *exceptionali ordine*[65] [sic] of the Cause of the Servant of God before the Sacred Congregation of Rites.

The Postulation consequently is assured not to perish. It is in sure and faithful hands. The impas-sioned and inconceivable opposition that delays its

---

[64]Circle of Popillius: in reference to Gaius Popillius Laenas, a Roman ambassador (later consul) who reportedly, in 168 BC, drew a circle in the sand around Antiochus IV Epiphanes of the Seleucid Empire, ordering him not to leave the circle until he had answered his question regarding the war with Egypt.

[65]*exceptionali ordine*: by exceptional means.

success, which would so want to make it impossible and which piously collects the *manure* of all ruminants of calumny in order to stone the *idlest* of men; that stupid and powerful opposition, the principal actors of which I will name, will not speak all alone at least and will not triumph in the sempiternal mutism of public consciousness. The future of that exceptional Cause which interests all peoples depends, moreover, at this moment, on a single man who can, with one word, annihilate that conspiration of reptiles. That man, he is the Vicar of Jesus Christ. SIX HUNDRED FIFTEEN Bishops[66] are at his feet, and behind them, all those who, in the Christian universe, represent the authority of virtue or the aristocracy of thought...

Now, God knows if time presses us! Here comes the fourth centenary of the Discovery. In an atheistic century and nevertheless as free as our own from apotheoses and simulacra, it is reasonable to conjecture that an extraordinary effort will be attempted to extend the nascent aureole of the apostle under the deluge of philanthropic and revolutionary dithyrambs. Catholics will judge whether some difficulties of procedure opposed to the Beatification of the greatest Christian hero of modern times can and should enter into the balance with the enormous evident interest of restituting to the Church a first-rate glory that is entirely its own and that his most abject enemies have undertaken to rob him of. It is worthy, in fact, of the Church, to protect its first-born and to

---

[66]Original footnote: Since the day of presentation by the Vice Postulator, the number of episcopal adherents has increased (November 1883).

make their memory be respected when they have ceased to wage battle and suffer for her. It is worthy of France, formerly called the eldest daughter of that Mother, and which has had the honor of requesting, *the first nation to do so*, that solemn reparation; it is very worthy of France to continue requesting it with cries and prayers. It is worthy, finally, of the universal Episcopate which has already so nobly interceded on behalf of the august Patriarch of transatlantic missions to recommence before the Roman Cathedra its eloquent importunity and to prolong until the day, verisimilously near, when the mystical Bride of the King of Glory, the Father of the Poor, will sing finally, on May 20, from atop its altars, the eternal Nativity of the Ambassador of Jesus Christ!

XIII

On Friday, October 12, 1492, Christopher Columbus took possession of the Island of San Salvador, in the name of Our Lord Jesus Christ, for the crown of Castille. He had barely set foot on that new land, first fruits of his discoveries, when planting the Cross[67] significatively and prostrating himself with adoration he said: "Lord, eternal and all-powerful God who, by your sacred Word, have created the firmament and the land and the sea! may your Name be blessed and

---

[67]Original footnote: It is not as a sign of possession that he erects that Cross everywhere, as the Protestant school pretends, but to announce Salvation, the Cross being, in his own words: principally the symbol of Our Lord Jesus Christ and the honor of Christianity. "Y principalmente por Señal de Jesuchristo Nuestro Señor y honra de la cristiandad." – Columbus' Journal, Wednesday, 12 December 1492.

glorified everywhere; may it be exalted, your Majesty, which has deigned to permit, by your humble servant, that your sacred Name should be known and preached in this other part of the world!"[68]

Those few lines will suffice for every Christian soul, however lacking in profundity he or she might be, to understand the absolute necessity of exceptional means. Christopher Columbus thanks divine majesty for having deigned to permit that, through him, his Name might be known and preached in *that other part of the world*. The enormous singularity of a similar act of grace is necessarily inaccessible to men of the XIXth century. One must needs ask oneself what that other part of the world could have been like in the eyes of men of the XVth century. There was, to begin with, the *Tenebrous Sea*, the frightening BAHR-AL-TALMET of the Arabs, that is to say a belt of abysses peopled by monsters compared to which the most horrible nightmares of infernal mysticism must have appeared benign and consoling. Beyond it was the Devil, despair, hell, absolute night and absolute absence of God. Christopher Columbus, who did not believe in the Tenebrous Sea because he had a premonition of the true shape of the Globe; Christopher Columbus, filled with his gifts and superior to his contemporaries in all natural and supernatural superiorities, did he see much more clearly than the common sort into the order of things historically contingent with his mission?

Doubtless, that marvelous man felt himself

---

[68]Original footnote: *Christopher Columbus*, by the Count Roselly de Lorgues, book 1, chap. VIII.

called to the translation of the Cross to a new world, he declared as much himself implicitly or explicitly in a hundred places. Doubtless, the feeling of his gigantic spiritual paternity filled the breast of that Abraham voyager in search of his unknown posterity. Doubtless also, he had to believe that that captive world would not be handed over to him without a fight, and his heroic soul counted on the God of the oppressed to decide his fortune. But the extraordinary injustice, the unprecedented ingratitude, the indefatigable persistence of misfortunes as he had never seen before and, above all, the supernatural, absolute, implacable insuccess of all his efforts – with the exception of the Discovery, – that there must have strangely astonished his soul, which was unique among the unique!

Whatever the gift of intuition that that passenger of Providence and Sorrow had, he who doubled the surface area of the earth, only to find he had no asylum there, he could not divine that the entire universe was going to attack him; he could not think that his head was so precious to be offered up as a holocaust, and that is precisely because it had to be, just as his prayer is so surprising. That other part of the world, as he said, belongs so much to the Demon that the plan to preach to it the name of God must have seemed like an apostolic vocation in hell. Also was it that he was practically alone in having that dream. Spain and Europe absolutely did not want that there should be *another* part of the world or that it should become the domain of Jesus Christ by its humble servant who had revealed it. They wanted, on the contrary, to assimilate it, like a prey, and to propagate themselves there in such a way that it was no longer possible to find anything else but Europe all over the earth. The ancient Latin civilization, folded over on itself in that narrow continent, polluted by its paganism, could finally straighten itself out and put itself at ease by stretching out its despicable legs over the New World. It was really just a matter of conquering souls, to tell the truth! Besides, given that they were in bed with the Devil, it was not necessary to stand on ceremony, everything was there for the taking, and the unfortunate Indians must have considered themselves happy to be enslaved and massacred by so superior a race!

As for Columbus, "the seas were tired of carrying him" and the continents no longer wanted to. Powerful men and women of the world played with that old driveler of fraternity and justice. The true fatherland of men, – it is their desire; and the desire of that apostle having been so perfectly disappointed, he found himself without a fatherland from then on, wandering by land and by sea, beaten by the waves, ridiculed by hurricanes, insulted by men, smashed by all the outraged forces of nature, without respite, without a home, and without bread on the table, collapsing under the universal anathema of ingratitude as if he had been the Cain of innocence!

Among the destinies that the world judges to be exceptional, had there ever been a single one to compare with that? And, given one presumes his holiness, and that it is now a question not just of a historical rehabilitation of the great Misunderstood man, but also of his beatification and of his canonization, what other way than by exceptional means could one take to arrive at setting on the altars a man whose probable sanctity is like a cry from the bottom of consciousnesses and which overwhelms, by the unprecedented remarkableness of his vocation, all foreseen categories in the august degrees of Urban VIII and Benedict XIV?

I will recount later the reception given to the project of introduction of the Cause by the Sacred Congregation of Rites, and I will keep myself here to conjecturing respectfully on what one might expect, in the future, from that venerable jurisdiction.[69] I want to limit myself for the moment to reproducing, in its interrogative format, a striking remark by the Count Roselly de Lorgues.

"Christopher Columbus is Exceptional to the degree," he said, "that the admission of his Cause to the Sacred Congregation of Rites, instead of making him greater in public opinion, as usually happens, raises in esteem the congregation itself. *It becomes illustrious by contact with him*. Let us not kid ourselves: however respectable that high tribunal might be, its judgments affect few men in the world. They let it function as it sees fit, without bothering themselves with its decisions. But this time, indifference gives way to deference and astonishment. How very imposing does it not appear, that Roman Areopagus, that summons to appear before it the greatest of men, him whom the Eternal chose as the instrument of his

---

[69]Sacred Congregation of Rites: a council or body established by Pope Sixtus V in 1588 and remaining in existence well into the late 19th century and afterwards, which had supervision over ceremonies, rites and liturgy, as well as processes of beatification and canonization, in the Roman Catholic Church.

Providence!

"That servant of God being Exceptional, can his Cause be of another nature than his person?"

I believe I have not forgotten anything essential in this rapid exposé of the Cause of Christopher Columbus. I will not push hability to the point of dissimulating that I have written these pages in the hope of giving him some admirers and *devotees*. If he should succeed only in obtaining a declaration of *Venerability*, the pursuance of an instance would still be necessary. Those are the very words of Cardinal Donnet, and it was also the sentiment of the learned archbishop of Genoa, Monseigneur Andrea Charvaz, immediate predecessor of the present titular. That prelate said with emotion to the Postulator: "As soon as Columbus is declared *Venerable*, most certainly some families of our mariners will start invoking him, and I have no doubt that it will produce miracles sufficient for proceeding on a regular path to his canonization."

After such authorities, I ask that I be permitted to add one last reflection.

When Christopher Columbus, the gentle apostle of the Verb, had to demand some extraordinary effort of his men, he said simply this to them: "*We owe it to God* to do such a thing," and with that he made goodwill enter their hearts. We others, we owe it to God to work extraordinarily for his Church, in these terrible times. That infinitely holy and sacred Church is, it also, a ship *en route* towards a really new world whose beauty must not perish. Presently, devoid of all human help, it battles with infinite tribulations against the most formidable tempest that the tenebrous genius of evil has ever raised against it at any time in history. Universal ingratitude is at its height and the spirit of revolt causes to desert, on a daily basis, a large number of servants whom one had the right of supposing faithful and incorruptible unto death. France, alas! Spain, Italy, and what remains still of Christian Germany, devoured and turned upside down by triumphant revolutionary cretinism, turn simultaneously against it and menace it with complete and irremediable shipwreck. Uniquely sustained by the promise of Jesus Christ, its distress has become so perfect, its destitution so total, and its abandonment so unprecedented that one is tempted to fear that God will not assuredly up and disappear one of these days; far from infidel Europe, the candelabrum and the torches. Lamentable voices rise from the breast of Christianity and from the breast of Anti-Christianity, and cry to us from every side that "there are no more saints in the Church," and it is really the most terrible thing to be pronounced on this world soaked in divine blood. We owe it to God then and to his Church to give the lie to that horrifying affirmation of the spirit of lies. Here then, I think, is the occasion for that magnificent refutation.

Hell's tactics are well understood. They have never changed and they obstinately refuse to adopt entirely new combinations of tactics in modern warfare. All the military genius of the Devil is reduced, in sum, to taking fortresses and massacring stragglers along the margin of paths, but he merely accepts against his better judgment, and only at the last extremity, battles ranged squarely on the plain. Ah, well! We must constrain him to battle in that way and we will then be assured of victory. Given that the Church has need of saints and that the unanimous voice of our first pastors warned us that they were only two paces away from us and, so to speak, in our midsts, marvelously accommodated to the genius of modern times by the exceptional speciality of his glory, – why wouldn't we go to meet him with enthusiasm and why wouldn't we oppose, like an invincible warrior chief, the more and more audacious enterprises of the enemies of Redemption?

The extreme importance of that determination is superabundantly indicated to us by the effort that they take to retard it and to get in our way. It is clear that the Prince of the World is frightened by Christopher Columbus. He wants none of that glory for the Church and for the Papacy. "Does one wish to know," asked the Count Roselly de Lorgues, "the effects of Catholic indifference with respect to that incomparable servant of God? Here they are: The clergy not claiming as one of its own that man who served it the most, impiety has turned him into its prey. Several years ago, the learned and courageous Abbot Margotti deplored the outrage committed against Columbus by the Piedmontese government, by placing his effigy opposite that of Cavour on their bank notes,[70] placing in this way the defender of pontifical royalty on the same level as that of the destroyer of temporal power. Since then, democratic Italians have undertaken to

---

[70]Columbus... Cavour... bank note: It is a bank note worth 10 lire with a bust of Cavour in the bottom left and a bust of Columbus in the bottom right.

confiscate that venerable personality. They have prostituted the name of Columbus, dragging it through the mud, giving it to schools of obligatory and laic instruction, taverns, estaminets, gambling dens. Sectarians of occult societies, agents of communism and the International, those violent enemies of the Papacy, have used it as a password. They have sullied as they please that sublime name, using it to found, who would have dared to believe it!... a lodge of Free Masons! Pursuing their abomination, they have attributed a role to Christopher Columbus in one of their favorite scenes of impiety. On March 17, 1872, they reserved a place of honor for him at the most solemn of civil burials that has ever been seen: that of the demoniacal chief of revolutionaries, the great hierophant of assassins, the frenetic Mazzini.

> "*They have placed on the hearse, next to the coffin, the portrait of the servant of God with those of the heresiarch Arnaldo da Brescia, the conspirator Cola di Rienzo, and the dark Machiavelli; and those impious funeral services didn't rile anyone.*

> "*One cannot stress it enough the extreme zeal that pushes enemies of the Papacy to take hold of that name of Columbus with all their strength, to confiscate for the benefit of their dark calendars that shining renown. On June 22, 1879, a democratic society of Turinese workers, more than 600 in number, came to Genoa to celebrate*

the anniversary of Mazzini's birth, the patriarch and pontiff of assassins, whom they call the Apostle, il apostolo, *as if they were referring to Saint Paul or Saint Andrew. Seen from a certain distance, that impious or grotesque pilgrimage surprises in a singular way. One might conjecture at first that the fatherland of Saint Catherine must have given to those incredible devotees the reception that was appropriate to them and whom it simply ignominiously sent packing. That is the opposite of what happened. One part of the municipality came before them, led by banners and music. The mayors of Genoa and of Turin reciprocally congratulated each other. One immense Masonic joy extended over the city. Brothers and friends opened their souls each to each. An extraordinary fervor was kindled on that day for the revolution and against God. Then they went to lay bronze garlands on Mazzini's tomb and Christopher Columbus' monument. Those two men have been thus united and confounded in the same apotheosis. The disciple of the incarnate Verb, the sublime Cross-Bearer of the* Tenebrous Sea, *the gentle patriarch of transatlantic missions, has received in his own fatherland the same infamous*

honor as the odious mystagogue of po-
litical cutthroats. He has been de-
clared his equal in merit, in glory, in
apostolate, and I heard only a single
voice that was raised for justice in the
middle of that diabolical concert. *On*
the following day, the 23rd, a new cele-
bration reassembled those energumen
at the theater of the Politeama *and, at*
the moment when the universal
Church chanted the first vespers of the
Nativity of the Precursor of Jesus
Christ, the Free Masonry of two Ital-
ian cities, convened in that august lo-
cation to celebrate the nativity of its
greatest man, gave discourses in
which the names of Mazzini and
Columbus were intertwined amorously
for the greatest jubilation of that noble
people who knows how to glorify like
that the heroism of its children!"[71]

And that is what ingratitude can yield. I will
not add my reflections to those dreadful lines which I
wanted to end with. It will have to suffice to remind
all Christians who still love "charity, truth, and justice" that October 12, 1892 will be the fourth anniversary of the discovery. It is easy to predict that, with
the passion of adoration that Godless peoples ordinarily possess, that centenary will be celebrated in an unprecedented manner by mariners the world over. We
are just about ten years away from that epoch. What

---

[71]Original footnote: *The Ambassador of God and Pius IX*, Plon,
1874.

will Catholicism do on that solemn day? "Without the behind-the-scenes machinations of some pious individuals," said again the Count Roselly de Lorgues, "who pretend to serve the interests of the papacy, the place of the servant of God in the Church would have already be authentically defined. And from the instant that, by introduction of the cause, the Holy See recognizes the Catholic glory of Columbus, the revolutionaries, atheists, positivists would no longer dare to appropriate him as one of their own. Those arrogant people have a horror of saints. They distance themselves immediately like Satan from the corpse of Moses before the Archangel St. Michael."

Other Books by the Publisher

Fanchette's Pretty Little Foot
by Restif de La Bretonne

Je M'Accuse...
by Léon Bloy

My Hospitals & My Prisons
by Paul Verlaine

Salvation Through the Jews
by Léon Bloy

Words of a Demolitions Contractor
by Léon Bloy

Cellulely
by Paul Verlaine

Flowers of Bitumen
by Émile Goudeau

Songs for Her & Odes in Her Honor
by Paul Verlaine

On Huysmans' Tomb
by Léon Bloy

Ten Years a Bohemian
by Émile Goudeau

The Soul of Napoleon
by Léon Bloy